W9-CDS-141

A 2180 242920 5

6/16

you can RENEW this item from
home by visiting our Website at
www.woodbridge.lioninc.org or by
calling (203) 389-3433

SALMON

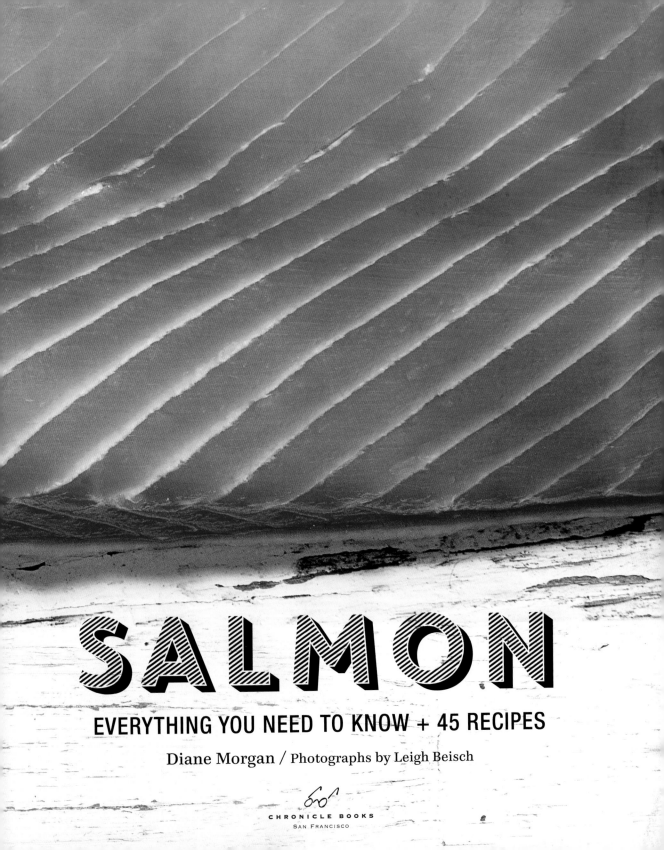

SALMON

EVERYTHING YOU NEED TO KNOW + 45 RECIPES

Diane Morgan / Photographs by Leigh Beisch

CHRONICLE BOOKS
SAN FRANCISCO

Text copyright © 2016 by Diane Morgan.
Photographs copyright © 2016 by Leigh Beisch.

All rights reserved. No part of this book may be reproduced in
any form without written permission from the publisher.

Library of Congress Cataloging-in-Publication Data available.

ISBN 978-1-4521-4835-9

Manufactured in China

Designed by Alice Chau

Food styling by Dan Becker
Prop styling by Ethel Brennan

The photographer wishes to thank Diane Morgan for writing
wonderful recipes and for thinking of us for this book; and
thank you to Alice Chau for also thinking of us for this project
and being so supportive of the creative process.

Chronicle books and gifts are available at special quantity
discounts to corporations, professional associations, literacy
programs, and other organizations. For details and discount
information, please contact our premiums department at
corporatesales@chroniclebooks.com or at 1-800-759-0190.

10 9 8 7 6 5 4 3 2 1

Chronicle Books LLC
680 Second Street
San Francisco, California 94107
www.chroniclebooks.com

*This book is dedicated to those who work hard
to preserve wild salmon stocks and their habitat.*

CONTENTS

INTRODUCTION

"Eating with the fullest pleasure—pleasure, that is, that does not depend on ignorance—is perhaps the profoundest enactment of our connection with the world. In this pleasure we experience and celebrate our dependence and our gratitude, for we are living from mystery, from creatures we did not make and powers we cannot comprehend."

—Wendell Berry

My first salmon cookbook was published in the spring of 2005. Two years earlier, with my book proposal accepted and a signed contract and an advance in hand, I decided it was important to travel in order to research salmon. My idea was to obtain a global perspective on the salmon industry—both farmed and wild—so I booked tickets to Norway, Scotland, and Alaska. I took along my husband, Greg, to serve as my logistics person, freeing me to study and take notes, and to make sure I didn't get lost, which I'm good at doing.

Norway is the birthplace of salmon aquaculture, so it made sense to travel there first. We visited the Norwegian Wild Salmon Centre (Norsk Villakssenter), on the banks of the Laerdalselvi, the longest river in Norway and the most famous salmon watercourse in the country. Opened by His Majesty King Harald on June 15, 1996, the Centre is dedicated to the preservation of wild salmon in Norway and offers extensive historical, scientific, and cultural exhibits for visitors. The Atlantic salmon stocks, severely depleted in the region due to overfishing, destruction of habitat, and the disease and inbreeding caused by farmed salmon, were the focus of scientists and conservationists working together to bring public awareness to these issues. It was there that I gained insights into the life and legends of Atlantic salmon and learned what Norway and the European Union were doing to protect, manage, and sustain the dwindling number of wild Atlantic salmon.

In Scotland, we visited an organic salmon farm within the Scottish Salmon Producers' Organisation, a trade association whose members are responsible for representing the industry in political, regulatory, technical, and media issues. The salmon farm, located near Ullapool on the far northwest coast of the Scottish Highlands, was established in 1977 and is the oldest independent fully integrated salmon farm in Scotland. The farm handles all stages of the production process, from egg to the initial processing of salmon fillets. To have a firsthand look at the farming operation, Greg and I were fitted with float suits and boated out to the net pens that were nestled in a protected sea loch. Not only was this a second-generation, family-run business but all of the employees we met were invested in the preservation of the environment and the care of the fish. They had grown up there, they were raising their children there, and they were feeding the salmon to their families.

The opportunity to see a "best practices" salmon farm was valuable and also hopeful, because the only salmon sold commercially throughout Europe are farmed salmon, and they typically come from a handful of large multinational corporations who control the aquaculture industry. There are important differences between salmon raised organically and salmon raised conventionally: Pen density is much lower for organically raised salmon, which optimizes the health and well-being of the fish. This lower density leads to less pollution of the seabed from undigested feed and feces, though this claim is being disputed. And new since 2010, all fish meal and oil used in organic farms must come from waste products of fisheries independently recognized as sustainable by the nonprofit Marine Stewardship Council (MSC), which operates a widely respected certification program.

In mid-May 2003, Greg and I visited Cordova, Alaska, shortly after the start of the salmon season for commercial fishermen. We spent time on an independent commercial salmon boat observing how sockeye and king salmon are caught by drift gill nets, the method of fishing used on the shallow channels of the Copper River Delta. Salmon fishing in Alaska is tightly regulated and managed for sustainability by the Alaska Department of Fish and Game, which is why Alaska is the global leader in the preservation of wild salmon stocks.

/////////////

Now, more than ten years after I researched and wrote my first salmon cookbook, I have been given the opportunity to write this new cookbook—to develop new recipes, revisit and update some readers' favorites, and once again focus deeply on the issues and challenges of both wild and farmed salmon. The reality, however, is that I never stopped watching the salmon industry. When *Salmon: A Cookbook* was published in 2005, I set up a Google alert on my computer so I could zero in on news articles covering farmed and wild salmon. I wanted to keep current with the science of aquaculture, the threats to wild salmon stocks and our oceans, the latest medical studies on the dietary benefits of omega-3 fatty acids, and how the marketplace for both wild and farmed salmon was evolving. In chapter 1 of this new book, I focus on the changes and advancements that have occurred in these areas over the past decade and also look at emerging topics, such as closed-containment salmon farming.

No matter how enticing the recipes and photographs might be, I encourage you to read chapter 2 before you start cooking. Here, I provide information on what to look for when shopping for salmon, including how to check for freshness and how to decode the labels on farmed and wild species. You'll also learn the best ways to store, freeze, and thaw salmon. Most important, this chapter contains essential techniques for salmon preparation, such as how to scale a fish, remove its gills, fillet it, and remove the skin and pin bones. I have also included two easy techniques that might appear "cheffy" at first glance, but I urge you to try them both and taste for yourself the amazing results. In just a few simple steps, the first one explains how to prepare a salmon fillet to achieve cracker-crisp skin, as it is served in the best restaurants. The second technique is brining. Although I have been a proponent of brining turkey and wrote about it extensively in my two Thanksgiving cookbooks, and even extended that same technique to pork, it had never occurred to me to brine salmon. Try it. The difference in taste and moistness is remarkable and well worth the very easy extra step.

Chapters 3 through 6—the recipe chapters—make up the heart of the book and are organized by technique (rather than by course). From appetizers to main courses, each chapter highlights a different approach to preparing salmon: raw and cured, on the stove top, in the oven, on the grill. Chapter 3 explores how to eat raw salmon safely as carpaccio and tartare and how to "cook" it with citrus to make ceviche; how to cure it with salt, sugar, and alcohol for gravlax; and how to pickle it with vinegar and spices in the style of herring. I include two of my favorite gravlax recipes, one traditional and the other less so, and both are delicious. In chapter 4, nearly every conceivable way to cook salmon on top of the stove appears: pan searing, braising, poaching, stove-top grilling, smoking, and stir-frying.

Chapter 5 turns up the heat with salmon in the oven. The recipes feature slow cooking, roasting, baking in parchment, broiling, searing in a cast-iron frying pan on the stove top followed by a high-heat finish in the oven, and even a low-tech sous-vide method. The latter is one modernist technique I am delighted to present.

In chapter 6, you'll need to fire up the grill. I have included recipes for a whole fish stuffed with aromatics, for using an alder plank for a wood-scented fillet that is a classic of the Pacific Northwest, and for wrapping fillets in cedar sheets for a Japanese-style presentation or in banana leaves for a Southeast Asian–inspired treat. You'll also discover salmon cubed and threaded onto skewers, formed into burgers, and cut into strips for tacos— all of them among my family's favorite

summertime dishes. Here, as in every recipe chapter, my goal is to help you build skills to achieve perfectly cooked salmon. With techniques mastered, the fun of improvising can begin.

I'm a huge fan of leftovers—salmon in particular—so I wanted to add a bonus chapter to the book. In chapter 7, you'll find recipes that utilize leftover salmon for breakfast, brunch, lunch, and dinner. With cooked salmon in the refrigerator, you can pull out a cast-iron frying pan and make hash, or whip up a frittata with spinach and goat cheese. Salmon gets reimagined in a chunky chowder with corn, stirred into risotto, or tossed with pasta. All are fast, easy, and flexible. Instead of forming burgers with salmon, make meatballs for a party and use the leftovers to make a salmon *bánh mi* sandwich. These leftovers feature big flavors and global tastes.

Everything about salmon fascinates me— its life cycle, the variety of species, the controversy and challenges regarding wild and farmed salmon, its health benefits, and its remarkable value as a protein source. As a cook, the versatility of salmon inspires me, it nourishes my body, and it brings me pleasure at the table. My global jaunt in search of the salmon story, which provided the context for my first book and deeply informed this new one, has been life transforming, connecting me to fishermen, biologists, conservationists, and aqua-culturists. Salmon is a glorious fish—a fish that we need to respect and protect so that it can provide us pleasure and sustenance forever.

CHAPTER 1:
ESSENTIALS

I am completely hooked on salmon. The legends and lore are captivating, the life cycle of salmon is fascinating, and the variety of species within the *Salmonidae* family is remarkable. And, as a food source, salmon is a superfood—a powerhouse of protein packed with marine-derived omega-3 essential fatty acids.

This opening chapter explores these topics, and I urge you, at some point, to step away from the stove or grill and focus a bit of time here. Settle into an easy chair with a cup of tea, or, hey, even a microbrew or a glass of pinot noir, and read about this glorious and complex fish.

Here I provide an overview of a salmon's life cycle. The amazing journey, migrating from freshwater streams, rivers, and tributaries out to sea, growing and maturing in salt water for several seasons, and then swimming great distances back to their natal rivers to spawn. These rhythms of nature bring us closer to understanding and respecting our food sources. In the same regard, learning about the different species of salmon shapes our connections to the seasons and makes for a more informed consumer when shopping for salmon at the market. For those who are able to source Pacific salmon, we welcome the first runs of sockeye salmon in May. King salmon typically peak by the middle of July, followed by the less-fatty coho salmon and cannery-favorite pink salmon later in the season. Sports fishermen will be ready any cool, overcast day in the fall to cast a line for steelhead salmon.

Caring about salmon as a valuable protein source involves understanding issues of sustainability, including gaining a global perspective on the challenges facing the salmon industry, aquaculture, and the health of our oceans. To be an informed and responsible consumer means preserving what nature so gloriously provides. And, speaking of health, I end this chapter writing about salmon and omega-3s—the queen of fats. Eating a diet rich in omega-3 fatty acids is good for our brains, heart, eyes, bones, and skin, as well as our longevity.

THE LIFE OF SALMON

Salmon are fantastical fish with complex, wondrous lives. They are anadromous, which means they are born in freshwater, migrate and spend most of their lives in salt water, and then return to freshwater to spawn. Their life cycle is truly extraordinary. It begins in the waters of a river and its tributaries or in a lake with an outlet river. Here, the adults mate and lay eggs—as many as three to five thousand of them. The female turns on her side and, by bending her body and striking with her tail, creates a depression in the gravel of the streambed. This spawning nest is called a redd. The female makes a series of redds and, in each, deposits a portion of her eggs, which are then fertilized by the male partner. After all the eggs have been deposited and fertilized, both female and male, with rare exception, age rapidly and die.

When the eggs hatch about four months later, the young fish, or alevins, consume their yolk sac, which takes four to six weeks, and then emerge from the redds. At this stage, they are called fry, and then later—a year after hatching—they are known as parr. The parr feed and grow in the stream until they are ready to begin their first migration down the tributaries to the river and finally out to sea. During this journey, the young fish undergo a complex set of physiological changes that prepares them for living in salt water. After these changes, they are referred to as smolts. Salmon live in the ocean from one to five years, eating—and being eaten—and growing until they reach sexual maturity. The returning adults undergo a reverse set of physiological changes, allowing them to migrate from salt water to freshwater. They regularly swim great distances to return to the river of their birth, where they spawn and then sometimes die, completing their life cycle.

What is it that directs salmon to travel from open ocean back to spawn and create the next generation in the same tributary or lake where they were hatched? Some scientists believe that salmon have a navigational sense similar to that of migratory birds. They also theorize that chemical imprinting during early development allows salmon to detect and home in on the unique chemical signature of not only the watercourse of their birth but also the very gravel bed in which they were conceived and from which they emerged to begin their lives. Understanding this life cycle, the interdependence of our environment, the rhythms of nature, and our need to preserve it informs us. We make choices about what we eat based on knowledge, respect, appreciation, and preservation.

ATLANTIC SALMON AND PACIFIC SALMON: KNOW YOUR SPECIES

Even though Atlantic and Pacific salmon look similar, are characteristically athletic in their ability to avoid predators and leap over waterfalls and rapids on the way back to their spawning grounds, and are in the same family, Salmonidae, along with trout and arctic char, they are classified in different genera. One of the key biological differences between Atlantic and Pacific salmon is that Atlantic salmon are iteroparous, that is, they do not die after returning to spawn in their natal streams and can return to the sea. Pacific salmon and other members of the *Oncorhynchus* genus are semelparous, with mature members of the population generally dying within a short time of spawning.

ATLANTIC SALMON

These belong to the genus *Salmo*, and within that genus there is only one species, *salar*, which means "leaper" in Latin. Mature wild Atlantic salmon average about 10 lb [4.5 kg], are about 30 in [76 cm] long, and are sleek and muscular, with steel-blue backs covered with tiny black crosses. They are silver below the lateral line, with white bellies, and their flesh is firm and deep pink. The range of wild Atlantic salmon once extended from New York's Hudson River all the way up the North Atlantic and arcing over to Russia's White Sea and down to the Douro River in Portugal. Many of these runs are now severely

reduced or extinct due to industrialization, habitat loss, pollution, and overfishing by commercial fleets. The only wild Atlantic salmon available are those caught by recreational fishermen, though conservationists and marine biologists dedicated to saving wild stocks are working hard to introduce Atlantic salmon back into their native waters. For now and the foreseeable future, all the fresh Atlantic salmon in the marketplace, apart from a minuscule amount of boutique wild Atlantic fish imported from Europe, are farmed.

PACIFIC SALMON

These belong to the genus *Oncorhynchus*, but unlike Atlantic salmon, the Pacific genus includes seven species, six of which are native to North America. The seventh, the masu or cherry salmon (*O. masou*), is found in the western Pacific waters off the coast of Japan, Korea, and parts of Taiwan. It is not detailed in this discussion.

THE CHINOOK (KING) SALMON (*O. tshawytscha*) is truly the "king" of all the Pacific salmon species, not only for its size but also for its economic value. The flavor and texture of the flesh are incomparable, and the heart-healthy, omega-3-rich fat often exceeds 20 percent, higher than any other wild fish. King salmon can weigh more than 100 lb [45 kg], but most weigh 15 to 20 lb [7 to 9 kg] and measure up to 36 in [91 cm] in length. Hefty in appearance, kings are blue-green on the back and the top of the head, with silvery sides and white bellies. They have black spots on the upper half of their body and tail, plus distinctive black lower gums. Their flesh ranges from off-white to pinkish red. The rarely caught white-fleshed king, whose food source consists of sardines and anchovies as opposed to shrimplike pink krill, have taken on a boutique status in the marketplace, where they are called "ivory salmon."

Kings range from Kotzebue Sound, Alaska, to Santa Barbara, California. Their season begins in mid-April in California; mid-May in Oregon, Washington, and British Columbia; and early June in Alaska. It typically lasts until late September and into October in a good year. Not as popular for farming as other species, farmed kings weigh 5 to 15 lb [2.3 to 7 kg].

COHO (SILVER) SALMON (*O. kisutch*) come close to chinook in flavor but are smaller, weighing from 8 to 12 lb [3.6 to 5.4 kg] and ranging from 18 to 24 in [46 to 61 cm] in length. Adult cohos are steel blue to pale green, with silvery sides and white bellies. They have white gums, small black spots on their backs, and are only lightly spotted at the top of the tail. The flesh is firmly textured and ranges from deep red to pinkish orange. Coho salmon occur naturally only in the Pacific Ocean and its tributaries, from northern Alaska to as far south as Monterey Bay, California, though the stocks in Oregon and California are classified as threatened under the Endangered Species Act. The best catches are made between July and September, with a peak in August. Coho salmon are also farmed and weigh 6 to 8 lb [2.7 to 3.6 kg] at harvest.

SOCKEYE (RED) SALMON (*O. nerka*) are long and slender, typically 5 to 10 lb [2.3 to 4.5 kg] at maturity, with most weighing about 6 lb [2.7 kg]. Their large, glassy penetrating eyes distinguish them from coho salmon in the wild. Sockeyes have spot-free forest-green backs, bright silver bellies, and look almost as smooth as glass, like they are set in gel, when freshly caught. They have pale gums that bear no teeth, unlike a king or coho. At the spawning stage, the head of the sockeye turns olive green while the body turns bright red. Although this is one of the reasons sockeyes are sometimes called "reds," the name is also due to the color of their flesh.

They have bright, deep orange flesh with a high fat content that makes them prized, distinctive, and delicious. Sockeye is the premium canned salmon variety and very popular for smoking. The fish range as far south as California, but they are most abundant from the Columbia River northward, with large concentrations in British Columbia and Alaska. The vast Bristol Bay watershed is responsible for 40 percent of all the sockeye salmon caught. Wild sockeyes that make it to market as unprocessed fish are typically available from late May to September.

THE PINK (HUMPBACK) SALMON (*O. gorbuscha*) is by far the most numerous of the Pacific salmon species, representing a little more than 50 percent of all the salmon caught in Alaska. Pinks are typically 18 to 24 in [46 to 61 cm] long and reach an average weight of 3 to 5 lb [1.4 to 2.3 kg]. They are steel blue to blue-green, with large black dots and silver sides. As the common name implies, the flesh is pale pink, lean, and fine textured, with a milder flavor than the other Pacific species. Pinks are widely used for canning, though those that make it to market unprocessed are typically sold whole—and at bargain prices.

CHUM (KETA OR DOG) SALMON (*O. keta*) are elongated and slim, usually measuring about 25 in [63.5 cm] in length and weighing about 10 lb [4.5 kg]. Their backs and upper sides are steel blue, without the fine black speckles of the other Pacific species, and they have silvery white bellies. During spawning season, they develop elongated teeth, which is why they were given the common name "dog." Outside of Alaska, chums are sometimes sold under the label "keta." The flavor, texture, and fat content of chums vary considerably depending on where and when the fish are caught. If chums are caught in the ocean when they are still actively feeding, their flavor and fat content are at their best. Chum salmon in this condition—silvery skinned, almost like coho, with reddish flesh—are labeled "silver brites" and command a higher price than those tagged "semi-brites" and "darks." As you might guess from the labeling, semi-brites have darker skin and paler flesh, and darks have the darkest skin and are noticeably paler and lower in fat. Chum salmon are commercially fished from Washington to Alaska, but can be found in the Arctic Ocean, as well as in the Okhotsk and Bering Seas. Japan's hatchery-based fishery accounts for the world's largest annual catch of chum salmon. Alaska comes in second, producing about 85 percent of the U.S. chum catch. The remainder are caught in Washington. Although chum salmon is sold fresh in supermarkets, its real market value is when it is processed and sold as salmon burgers or sausages.

STEELHEAD SALMON (*O. mykiss*) and rainbow trout used to be identified by the Latin name *Salmo gairdneri* and were considered part of the same genus as Atlantic salmon and various trout of the Atlantic basin. However, scientists have long argued that rainbow trout, and especially steelhead salmon, have anatomical and behavioral traits that more closely match the Pacific salmon. In 1989, the American Fisheries Society approved and adopted this reclassification. Rainbow trout and steelhead are extremely similar. The single major difference is that steelhead are a sea-going fish and rainbow trout inhabit only freshwater. Steelhead salmon are 12 to 18 in [30.5 to 46 cm] in length and usually weigh 5 to 9 lb [2.3 to 4 kg], though recreational fishermen have caught steelhead as large as 36 lb [16 kg]. They are silvery, with a number of small black spots. The flesh is usually bright red and rich or pink to white, depending on the diet. Steelhead and rainbow trout are rated two of the top five sport fish in North America. On Washington's

Olympic Peninsula, the Quinault Indian tribe has spent the last three decades developing a successful hatchery program of wild steelhead stocks and are harvesting a plentiful, commercial supply available in Northwest markets. In other parts of the world, fish labeled "steelhead" are rainbow trout raised on farms in salt water.

WILD VERSUS FARMED SALMON: A GLOBAL PERSPECTIVE

Free-living Atlantic and Pacific salmon have been a valuable food source for millennia. Hunter-gatherer groups resident along the coastal waters and major tributaries of North America caught what they needed while preserving the waterways that produced their harvest. Evidence exists of indigenous people having iconic relationships with salmon some twelve thousand years ago, from the Tlingits in Alaska to the Wyampum along the mighty Columbia River in the Pacific Northwest. Across the Atlantic, one of the oldest habitation sites in Ireland was discovered in 1972 at Mount Sandel, a bluff overlooking the River Bann. Careful analysis of evidence dating to before 7000 B.C.E. has shown that hunter-gatherers there erected huts, gathered nuts, hunted boar, and speared salmon.

Fast-forwarding through the centuries, legislation to protect salmon was enacted by William the Lion, who ruled Scotland from 1165 to 1214. In the thirteenth century, Norwegian legislation known as the Gulating Law and the National Law of Magnus Lagabøter regulated fair fishing conduct. During the Industrial Revolution, pressures on European waterways, habitat destruction, and pollution severely compromised the survival of salmon. Up until about 1800, the Thames, the longest watercourse in England, was an excellent salmon river. Pollution decimated the salmon—the last salmon was caught in 1833—and by 1855, the river was so contaminated that no fish could survive. A similar tale is true of the Rhine River in Germany. Up until the end of the nineteenth century, the Rhine was considered the best salmon river in Europe. In the early 1900s, the salmon disappeared because of hydroelectric development, and industrial pollution. The same pressures for manufacturing, development, and exploitation of energy resources were taking place in North America. Dams were being built, rivers were being polluted, and salmon populations were declining and, in some cases, becoming extinct.

As commercial fishermen became better skilled and better equipped, even more pressure was put on salmon stocks. In the absence of international regulation, the amount of salmon caught led to overfishing, without concern for the sustainability of either the fish or future fishermen. Not enough salmon were making it back to their natal rivers to spawn, in order to continue their natural life cycle. The demand for salmon exceeded the supply, which led to the beginnings of salmon farming.

PACIFIC SALMON

Alaska, home to abundant stocks of salmon, is the only state in the nation whose constitution explicitly mandates that all fish, including salmon, "shall be utilized, developed, and maintained on the sustained yield principle." As a result, Alaska's wild salmon fishery ranks as the healthiest and best managed in the world. There are no salmon farms in Alaska. All Alaska salmon are wild, living in their natural habitat, growing to adulthood at their own pace, and eating marine life, which in turn colors each variety of salmon to its own hue. During the salmon season, biologists use sonar to assess the returning salmon at

key streams and rivers. Regulating and managing the salmon runs ensure that spawning salmon return in sufficient numbers to produce future generations. Alaska also strictly regulates fishing. A limited number of licensed fishermen using regulated gear are allowed to fish in state waters up to three nautical miles offshore for restricted periods of time.

The salmon populations in Washington, Oregon, and California experienced some of the same pressures that befell European salmon stocks. Demand for hydroelectric power led to dams being built on key salmon rivers such as the Columbia, which divides Oregon and Washington. The development of urban and agricultural watersheds resulted in the polluting of rivers and streams. The consequence of these compounding factors has caused salmon populations to decline, and in some instances, become extinct in all three states.

So far, salmon aquaculture has been limited to a few sites in Washington. Oregon's coast isn't well suited to salmon farming (thank goodness!), as ocean net pens need both a constant rush of water to flush waste and the relative protection of a large bay. And, to the best of my research, California does not have open-net-pen salmon farms on its coastline. However, all three states and Alaska have extensive fish hatcheries that raise young salmon (eggs, fry, and juveniles) that are released in the wild. At this point, 70 to 80 percent of wild-caught salmon and steelhead in the Pacific Northwest originated in fish hatcheries. Biologists focused on wild salmon stocks see the benefits that salmon hatcheries can provide, but they also know that reliance on hatcheries as a substitute for the conservation of wild populations is a risky long-term conservation strategy.

Finally, the newest pressures on salmon habitat in southern Oregon and northern California have come from the growth of the marijuana industry. In January 2014, biologists at the National Oceanic and Atmospheric Administration (NOAA) released a report citing the unregulated use of fertilizers and stream-sucking irrigation systems by marijuana growers and the risk they pose to Oregon and California rivers, where chinook and other salmon swim.

ATLANTIC SALMON

In the 1950s, commercial fishermen began using sonar and drift nets to catch a record number of salmon gathering in the sea around Greenland and the Faroe Islands. The salmon were migrating from rivers in the United States, Canada, and Europe. Without regulation, the life cycle of the Atlantic salmon returning to their natal waters to spawn was interrupted, and it didn't take many years before the annual numbers crashed, resulting in the collapse of wild Atlantic salmon stocks.

Early recognition of this overfishing led pioneers to start researching and developing salmon farms in the 1960s. By the early 1970s, the industry was well under way in Norway in an effort to meet the growing demand for salmon in the marketplace. Scotland soon followed. Both of these areas were attractive as locations for fish pens because of the stretch of coastline, much of it protected from storms. Sheltered coastal waters warmed by the Gulf Stream, with nearby rivers providing the fresh-water needed to operate fish hatcheries, have also been ideal for growing salmon. By 1985, technology had evolved so that farmers could raise almost 200 tons of salmon in pens that produced only one-third of that amount the year before. As profits soared, a gold rush of sorts ensued.

By 1986, approximately 635 salmon farms produced 45,675 tons of salmon; by 1990, production had grown to 146,000 tons.

With a glut of salmon on the market, prices fell. Salmon farmers from Scotland and Ireland accused the Norwegians of dumping salmon on the market below production costs, which led to an investigation by the European Union. As government restrictions were put into place, large aquaculture companies began exporting technology, equipment, and financing to other countries, the largest of which were Canada, the United States, and Chile.

////////////

Today, with both steady growth and rising demand in the market, aquaculture overall accounts for almost half of all the salmon destined for human consumption. In 2013, the total supply of all farmed salmon was almost two million tons. In the same year, the total catch of wild salmon (with pink, chum, and sockeye the most common species) was just under one million tons. What is new in the industry since I wrote my first salmon cookbook in 2005 is how the fish is processed. That work is now done with cheaper labor costs. Instead of processing all the fish locally, about 25 percent of the total catch of wild salmon from the United States, Russia, and Japan is exported as whole frozen fish to China, where it is processed much less expensively than is possible in the country of origin. It is then re-exported as frozen fillets.

The challenges of wild versus farmed salmon are both environmental and economic. Salmon farming, like most intensive forms of producing food, has significant environmental costs. Escapement is a huge issue. Large numbers of salmon escape from sea pens both routinely and in severe weather. Interbreeding of escaped salmon undermines the genetic robustness of wild salmon and also infects wild salmon with parasites and diseases. In British Columbia, escaped Atlantic salmon, a farmed species not native to Pacific waters, have populated a number of rivers. Diseases and infestations can spread rapidly to fish raised in overcrowded sea pens. Fish farmers combat these outbreaks using antibiotics, often resulting in disease-resistant bacteria turning up in the intestines of farmed fish. Sea lice, which were rarely found on the scales of wild juvenile salmon in the past, are now regularly seen on them. Uneaten feed and feces from salmon accumulate beneath the sea pens, contaminating the water, depleting oxygen levels, and releasing noxious gases in decomposition.

New technology is changing some of these aquaculture practices for the better. Although currently used in only a few sites, a closed containment system with an impermeable barrier that physically separates the fish from the external environment is a promising direction. It prevents the transmission of diseases and parasites, eliminates escapement issues, requires fewer chemicals, and uses less feed, which lowers the pressure on wild fish used in feed. It also treats waste within the system, rather than discharging it into the ocean, thus virtually halting pollution of the marine environment. Unfortunately, the investment dollars and cost per fish are keeping this system limited for now.

Another challenge of aquaculture, focused on salmon specifically, is the amount of little fish it takes to produce the feed to grow the big fish in a fish-farming operation. Historically, fish feed has been made from fish meal and fish oil from forage fish such as anchovies and sardines. Annually, these fish represent nearly one-third of the global fisheries' catch, and they are mostly processed into fish meal and fish oil used in fish, poultry, and livestock feeds.

The ongoing concern of biologists and environmentalists is that this catch rate is not sustainable. The fish feed industry has replaced these marine raw materials with agricultural commodities that mimic the omega-3s found in the small fish. Products such as soy, sunflower, wheat, corn, beans, peas, rapeseed oil, and poultry by-products (in Chilean and Canadian aquaculture) are combined and used in place of marine-based feed. Fish meal and other raw materials of animal origin have a more complete amino acid profile than protein of vegetable origin and generally have a higher protein concentration. That means that completely replacing fish meal poses a big challenge. The optimization strategy for this industry is to grow a healthy fish fast at the lowest possible production cost. Some aquaculturists are focused on premium feed for their salmon and are branding their salmon products accordingly.

As consumers, we are the responsible ones. We can vote with our pocketbooks. It is our job to understand the true cost of a $7.99-per-1-lb [455-g] salmon fillet in a broad context. Buying wild salmon, or buying responsibly farmed salmon from a farm with a recognized certification of quality, costs more, but it is the only way to avoid contributing to the overwhelming environmental and economic impact caused by these agrochemical fish farms. We need to ask questions and, hopefully, to buy only fish that meet a high standard of excellence, whether at the grocery store or in a restaurant. I recognize I am privileged living in the Pacific Northwest because I have easy access to wild salmon, so my position is, "I eat wild to save wild." It's my way of voting.

SALMON AND HEALTH: THOSE WONDERFUL OMEGA-3S

Let's make a twist on the Dutch proverb that says, "A land with lots of herring can get along with few doctors." Why not, "A body with a bountiful supply of omega-3 fatty acids can get along with few doctors"? Although it is perhaps less poetic, it is nonetheless a truthful statement. Just ask the researchers focused on heart disease, cancer, diabetes, clinical nutrition, eye health, and dementia. They understand that a daily regimen rich in long-chain (highly unsaturated) omega-3 fatty acids (eicosapentaeonic acid, or EPA, and docosahexaenoic acid, or DHA) protects against a slew of life-threatening diseases. Optimal health means a diet high in these critical fats.

Optimal Health

Salmon is a superfood, a powerhouse of high-quality, incredibly delicious, flavorful protein that is packed with marine-derived omega-3 essential fatty acids (EFAs). It is also a valuable source of vitamin D, along with vitamins A, E, B6, and B12, and of niacin and riboflavin. Two to three servings a week of oil-rich fish such as salmon are recommended for an optimal diet. Many clinical trials have used doses of 1000 to 3000 mg of EPA and DHA per day with no adverse effects. The U.S. Food and Drug Administration (FDA) has said it sees no risk from intakes up to 3000 mg of EPA and DHA per day, while the American Heart Association recommends doses up to 4000 mg per day under a physician's supervision. Here is how to translate that

to eating salmon: there are 2000 mg of omega-3s in a 3½-oz [100-g] serving of king salmon; 1300 mg in the same-size portion of coho salmon; and 1200 mg in an equivalent amount of sockeye salmon. If eating an abundance of anchovies appeals, you will be happy to know that you are consuming 3300 mg of omega-3s in 3½ oz [100 g] of these little fish.

Heart Health

Eating a diet rich in omega-3 fats helps lower blood triglycerides and cholesterol levels, contributing to heart health. Omega-3s also help maintain the flexibility of arteries and veins (because EFAs act as blood thinners), strengthen cardiac muscles, and aid in repairing damage to cardiovascular tissue. The benefits of reduced blood pressure, lowered cholesterol, and prevention of hardened artery walls mean significant protection from heart attack, stroke, arrhythmia, and hypertension.

Anti-Inflammatory

Researchers believe the anti-inflammatory effects of omega-3 fats help reduce the symptoms of autoimmune diseases such as rheumatoid arthritis and lupus and prolong the life of those who suffer from them. In addition, calcitonin, a protein hormone found in the thyroid-like glands of salmon, has been extracted and developed pharmaceutically for the treatment of osteoporosis, helping to improve bone density and strength.

Eye Health

Studies, especially the large and ongoing Nurses' Health Study, have shown that people who eat a diet rich in marine-derived omega-3s have a significantly lower risk of macular degeneration, a chronic eye condition that leads to loss of vision. DHA is the dominant fatty acid in our retinas, so boosting our diet with these good fats promotes eye health and is important to the synapses that connect brain cells and our eyes' light receptors.

Brain Health

Our brains are fatty. Their tissues average 50 percent fatty acids by weight. Omega-3 fatty acids are critical to brain function and help regulate mood-related signals. Evidence suggests that eating salmon and other marine-derived omega-3 fatty foods several times a week may reduce the risk of depression, ADHD, schizophrenia, bipolar disorder, dementia, and Alzheimer's disease.

A Natural Facelift

No need for snipping and tightening our skin. Eating a diet rich in omega-3s reportedly helps fight wrinkles, making the skin look and feel younger—the equivalent of a nutritional facelift!

Longevity

And finally, we can live more than two years longer with a diet rich in omega-3s! From the Harvard Gazette, an online publication of the Harvard School of Public Health, comes this statement:

Older adults who have high blood levels of omega-3 fatty acids—found almost exclusively in fatty seafood—may be able to lower their overall mortality risk by as much as 27 percent and their mortality risk from heart disease by about 35 percent, according to a new study from the Harvard School of Public Health (HSPH) and the University of Washington. Researchers found that older adults who had the highest blood levels of the fatty acids lived, on average, 2.2 years longer than those with lower levels.

"Although eating fish has long been considered part of a healthy diet, few studies have assessed blood omega-3 levels and total deaths in older adults," said lead author Dariush Mozaffarian, associate professor in the Department of Epidemiology at HSPH. "Our findings support the importance of adequate blood omega-3 levels for cardiovascular health, and suggest that later in life these benefits could actually extend the years of remaining life."

CHAPTER 2:
PREPARATION PRIMER

My hope is that you will take the time to read through this chapter before you begin tackling the recipes. This is where I introduce you to the fundamental techniques for preparing and cooking salmon. I provide detailed directions on how to gut and clean a whole salmon. For those who fish, this will likely be a handed-down skill; for those shopping at a quality fish market, the fishmonger, if asked, will likely do this for you. That said, at the height of the season, markets often stock whole fish at better prices, and prepping the salmon yourself saves you money.

Shopping for salmon in the fish case means reading the labels that should specify whether the fish is fresh or has been previously frozen, its country of origin, and whether the salmon is farmed or wild. Beyond that, there is lots of confusing, unregulated marketing language to learn, and that is covered in this chapter.

Once the salmon is brought home, storing it to maximize freshness is key. Freezing and thawing salmon is discussed here, as well as proper refrigeration. In addition, basic preparation techniques are detailed—scaling a fish, removing the gills, filleting and skinning salmon, removing pin bones, and portioning the fish. These are the building blocks for all the recipes in the book and, for that matter, any salmon recipe you choose to prepare.

For most of us, obtaining raw salmon to prepare at home begins at the grocery store or fish market rather than out at sea in a boat. That makes understanding seafood labeling critical to savvy shopping. In 2005, the federal government, under the jurisdiction of the United States Department of Agriculture (USDA), developed mandatory labeling rules for the seafood industry designed to inform consumers whether the seafood they are about to purchase is wild or farmed and notify them of its country of origin. Although this labeling program was a good first start, the rules failed to cover much of the seafood that is sold today. For example, "processed" seafood, such as frozen salmon burgers or breaded fish fillets, are exempt from the program, which leaves more than 50 percent of all seafood sold in the United States without labels. Wholesale markets, such as those selling directly to restaurants, are also exempt. With all this flabby labeling, the consumer is tasked with buying seafood from a trusted and reliable source. I suggest you make friends with your fishmonger! Once you have purchased your seafood, bring it home and store it properly; or better yet, cook it that night for dinner. (Information on storing and freezing begins on page 35.)

The recipes in this book call for individual serving-size portions, for a whole side (fillet) of salmon, or for a whole fish. In this chapter, you will find directions on everything from how to fillet a fish and how to remove pin bones to scaling, skinning, portioning servings, and even skin-drying and brining. Mastering all of these techniques—none of which is difficult—will not only help build your culinary skills but also your kitchen confidence.

I read chefs' cookbooks less for the recipes and more for the techniques they use. That's how I came to learn about drying the fish skin to achieve a crackly, waferlike crispness. It's a brilliant idea, and I must thank Thomas Keller for telling his readers how to do it. I also spent time researching and testing the value of brining fish before cooking it, and I'm now hooked on that technique, too. You'll find the recipe at the end of this chapter.

Most people who have painted a house say that 80 percent of the work is in the prep, and that's true of fish cookery, too. This chapter provides all the prep tips and techniques you'll need to prepare great salmon dishes. Each recipe in the chapters that follow specifies how the salmon is to be prepped in the ingredients list. For instance, a recipe might call for a whole side of salmon to be skinned and the pin bones removed. This chapter explains how to do that detailed prep work. Of course, you could ask the fishmonger to fillet a side of salmon for you; however, only one with extra time on his or her hands will pull pin bones. Just like painting, where the time taken to spackle and sand produces a quality job, mastering pin-bone removal, skinning, and skin-drying techniques results in cooked fish any chef would be proud to serve.

FRESH-CAUGHT SALMON

I caught my first fish in late spring of 2003 when I went to Alaska to research wild salmon. I was visiting the Copper River watershed with my husband and friends in tow. We hired a guide and went out on a small boat for a fun day of salmon fishing. But instead of hooking a salmon, I caught a 75-lb [34-kg] halibut! With much encouragement, direction, and all the power my body and overtaxed limbs could muster, I reeled in that huge fish. The serenity of the wait, the thrill of the tug on the line, and the struggle to spool in a big fish were exhilarating and addictive.

Although fishing is not my sport of choice (I prefer hiking), that experience helped me to understand firsthand why folks fish. Plus, there is nothing like hooking a salmon, a steelhead, a big halibut, or, for that matter, any good-eating fish and then cooking it just hours later. Seasoned anglers can skip over my description of going from catch to gutting because this is second nature to them, but for me, it was a crucial learning step in preparing a fish for a meal. And if you are going to fish, you've got to know how to clean and gut your catch. If you shop for salmon rather than fish for salmon, skip ahead to the section on shopping tips.

CLEANING AND GUTTING A WHOLE SALMON

As soon as you pull the fish out of the water, strike it on the back of the head with a rock, hammer, or club. This usually renders it unconscious. The temporary stiffening of the muscles following death is called rigor mortis. A fish should be processed either before or after rigor, as handling it during rigor can cause the flesh to gap.

When you are ready to process the fish, position it so the belly is facing you. Slip a sharp knife in the anal opening just deep enough to cut through the flesh. Make a vertical cut all the way up from the anus to the operculum (the cover over the gills). Drain the blood and then spread open the abdominal cavity. Reach in and remove all the entrails. Rinse the cavity of the fish with cold running water to free it of blood, being sure to get all the blood out of the tissues.

Now, cut off and discard the fins, angling your knife and taking care to not tear the skin. If you want to leave the head on, immediately place the fish on ice. If you prefer to remove the head, place a knife right behind the gills on a slightly angled line perpendicular to the spinal column. Cut through on both sides, separating the head (with gills attached) from the body, and then place the fish on ice. If you want to make salmon stock, rinse the head, remove the gills (see page 36), and place the salmon head on ice, as well.

SHOPPING FOR SALMON

Whether shopping for fish, vegetables, fruits, dairy, meat, or poultry, the key is to buy fresh, well-cared-for foods. In the best-case scenario, you are buying locally and seasonally, to make the connection between the grower or producer and the consumer. Living in Portland, Oregon, I can do that. At my local farmers' market, I buy in-season, Oregon-caught fresh salmon directly from the fisherman. I know how lucky I am, but I also know that, in this global marketplace, Copper River salmon caught one day off the shores of Cordova, Alaska, can be shipped overnight to restaurants and high-end fish markets all over the world. I know that farmed salmon raised in Chile, Norway, or off the coast of Scotland can be shipped overnight to global markets, as well. Here is how to use your senses to make sure that the fish you buy is fresh.

The first rule of shopping for fresh fish, whether at a supermarket, a small corner fish store, or a specialty market with a fish counter, is to get to know your fishmonger. If you will be shopping for fish often, introduce yourself, ask questions, become a regular. Always ask when a shipment of fish arrived, whether it has been frozen (not necessarily a bad thing), and where it came from. I like to shop in markets where the fish are on ice in a refrigerated glass case, where the counters and cases look clean, and where the fish are protected from direct sun, flies, and other possibly harmful conditions. I try to avoid fish sold in prewrapped packages. And if I walk into a market that has a strong fishy odor, rather than smelling like the sea, I walk right out.

Now, look at an individual fish. Is it moist and glistening? Is the skin silvery and bright? Are the eyes protruding, bright, and clear? If you are shopping for fillets, do the fillets look moist and freshly cut rather than flat and browned at the edges? If the fish looks good visually and you pick out a fillet for the fishmonger to weigh, feel free to ask to smell it. Fresh fish doesn't smell; there is no fishy odor. Anyone selling top-quality fish should be delighted you asked. If you feel shy about asking, just stand close to the scale as the fish is being weighed and take a whiff. Touch is important, too. If you are buying a whole fish or even a whole side of salmon, ask to touch the skin. A gentle nudge with your fingertip will let you know whether the fish is resilient and firm rather than mushy. Also, ask to see the gills; they should be bright pink or red. If the gills are pale or brownish, the fish is old. Finally, if you do establish a "regular customer" relationship with your fishmonger and you're happy, be sure to give feedback. "The fillets of salmon I bought last week were terrific; I grilled them just the way you suggested." It's all about caring at every level in the chain of food processing and marketing.

LABELING

Along with knowing how fresh the fish is, consumers rightfully want to know, now more than ever, where the fish is from and how it was raised. A story featured in the December 2011 edition of *Consumer Reports* identified widespread mislabeling of seafood sold at retail outlets and in restaurants. The cited study found that nearly 50 percent of the seafood tested in the New England area was incorrectly labeled. In 2013, Oceana, the largest international advocacy organization focused solely on ocean conservation, released a report on nationwide seafood fraud. With regard to salmon, the second-most-consumed fish in the United States, mislabeling was higher in restaurants (20 percent) and sushi venues (18 percent) than in grocery stores (5 percent). Salmon labeled as "wild salmon" was actually farmed salmon 27 percent of the time.

Why is this happening? Seafood commands a dear price in the market, and selling lesser fish at a premium price means bigger profits. If you think about it, it's an easy swap out for the less-than-reputable retailer or restaurateur. Fish, especially fully filleted fish, lose most of their distinguishing features when processed. Filleted fish, portioned fish, and especially fish turned into burgers, skewers, or sausages are hard for the average consumer to identify. Given the previous statistics on fraud, salmon burgers labeled or advertised as wild may actually be made from farmed salmon. Trust is key here. Shop at a trustworthy market, buy directly from a fisherman if you can, and ask questions at a restaurant. Finally, learn about the fish you like to eat. Learn the names of the species, such as king, coho, or sockeye for Pacific salmon, and learn the marketing names, the seasonality of the fish, and, best of all, eat it often enough to distinguish how it should taste.

For shopping for every type of seafood, I highly recommend you download the Monterey Bay Aquarium Seafood Watch guides on your smartphone or tablet. It is complete, up-to-date information that identifies specific fish and shellfish as a best choice, good alternative, or a specimen to avoid completely due to fishing practices, environmental factors, or sustainability issues. The list that follows will help you understand the often-confusing labels that appear on the little white signs stuck next to fillets indicating the origin of the fish and whether it is wild or farmed.

Organic

Most salmon labeled "organic" is actually farmed salmon originating from the North Atlantic, off the coasts of Ireland, Nova Scotia, and Scotland. Europe has had organic-certifying agencies in place for over fifteen years. Salmon farms with organic certification must operate in adherence with a strict set of standards.

Certified Organic

You should not see any salmon, or for that matter any fish or seafood, labeled "certified organic." The USDA, which governs organic rules in this country, has not yet set standards for aquatic species. The USDA organic seal applies only to crops and animals raised on land that meet strict federal guidelines.

All-Natural Farm-Raised Salmon or Environmentally Sustainable Salmon

This is unregulated marketing language that pertains to farmed salmon. As consumer concern for the environment and the quality of the fish continues to grow, smaller aquaculture businesses are responding and adopting environmentally friendly and responsible aquatic-farming practices. Stocking densities are reduced, the feed is organic or plant based, the salmon are raised without the use of antibiotics, the pigment used in the feed is from a natural source, and the use of pesticides to treat sea lice is strongly restricted. In addition, a relatively new method of salmon farming involves growing fish in tanks in inland locations away from the native habitat of wild fish stocks. This is a promising development in aquaculture, though it is also more expensive than raising salmon in open net pens in protected ocean coves.

Conventionally Farmed Salmon

Typically, Atlantic salmon is farm raised by large multinational corporations using dense stocking practices, nonorganic feed, antibiotics to maintain the health of the salmon, and pesticides to control disease. Almost always the least expensive of all salmon sold, these fish most often come from Europe, British Columbia, Chile, and U.S. coastal states.

Boutique Branding of Farmed Salmon

Aquaculture producers trying to distinguish their farmed salmon in the marketplace—because of the environmentally sensitive and, in some cases, patented practices they follow—have branded their salmon and sought approval from seafood watchdogs like the Monterey Bay Aquarium Seafood Watch program. Among them is Verlasso, a proprietary brand of AquaChile, which is the largest producer of farmed salmon in Chile. Verlasso has received a "good alternative" recommendation from the Monterey Bay Aquarium program. Following is the aquarium's detailed summary illustrating how cautious and focused these watchdog groups are on educating the consumer.

> *Verlasso was given a 'good alternative' designation because it uses a genetically modified yeast as a feed ingredient, thereby reducing its reliance on fishmeal and fish oil from wild fish. The salmon are farmed at lower densities than typical industry standards, and while chemical use is lower than the norm in Chile, antibiotic and pesticide use for Verlasso remains a high concern.*

> *Despite the open nature of its net pens, Verlasso has demonstrated an improvement upon the issues surrounding pollution and habitat damage. Atlantic salmon are not native, but studies show these salmon are very unlikely to establish self-sustaining wild populations in Chile. While disease has caused production problems in Chile as a whole, the potential effects on wild Chilean fish are not currently a high concern and therefore the risk of impacts from both escape and disease events are now considered moderate. Verlasso Salmon is sold in the United States as the brands Verlasso and Verlasso Harmoniously Raised Fish.*

Wild Salmon

These are salmon that are caught in their natal waters by commercial or tribal fishermen using the troll, drift-gill-net, or purse-seine fishing method, all of which are tightly regulated by state fishery management agencies.

Wild-Caught Salmon

A campaign to boost the image of Pacific salmon caught off the coast of California, Oregon, and Washington had to back off from using the word *wild* because fish activists objected, as many of the salmon caught off the Pacific coast are reared in hatcheries. These fish are now labeled "wild-caught salmon." In Alaska, hatchery-reared salmon account for about 30 percent of the catch. In the lower forty-eight states, hatcheries account for more than 50 percent of the salmon caught.

STORING SALMON

What any fisherman worth his salt will tell you is that keeping freshly caught fish clean and iced, as well as quickly processing it, is critical to quality and, of course, safety from spoilage. Ideally, buy fish on the day you plan to eat it. If you must store fish for a day, or two at the most, wrap it carefully and put it in the coldest part of the refrigerator. If the fish is enclosed in butcher paper, place it in a lock-top plastic bag or rewrap it tightly in plastic wrap. (Salmon fillets and steaks will get water spotted if in direct contact with water or ice.) Fill a deep pan or bowl with ice or, better yet, use reusable gel ice packs, and place the wrapped fish on top. Store it on the bottom shelf or the back of a lower shelf in the refrigerator. (If using ice, drain off the melted water and add more ice as needed.)

FREEZING SALMON

You must take special precautions in order to freeze salmon successfully. How you wrap your fish and the temperature at which you store it are critical. For the last five years, I have had the opportunity to buy salmon directly from a fisherman. I purchase 75 lb [34 kg] each season and ask the processor to cut the salmon into whole sides or 1- to 2-lb [455- to 910-g] fillets and vacuum seal the packages. The salmon is flash frozen and airfreighted to me. I have a manual-defrosting freezer that maintains the fish just below 0°F [-18°C]. The fish keeps beautifully for almost nine months. (Manual-defrosting freezers are better than self-defrosting ones because the process of self-defrosting dries out frozen foods more quickly.)

Vacuum-sealed packaging is ideal. If you fish, have generous friends who fish, or are able to purchase high-quality salmon in season and want to freeze it, think about either purchasing a small vacuum sealer or making friends with a butcher or fishmonger and paying them to vacuum pack the fish for you. Otherwise, wrap the fish as tightly as possible (without air pockets) in several thicknesses of plastic wrap, place it in a freezer-strength lock-top plastic bag, squeeze out the air in the bag, and freeze the fish. If you have a chest freezer or upright freezer that will keep the fish below 0°F [-18°C], the salmon should be fine for up to nine months. If you are storing the salmon in the freezer compartment of a refrigerator, plan to use it within one month.

THAWING SALMON

The best way to thaw salmon is to place the unopened package in a bowl or pan in the refrigerator. Fillets or a side of salmon usually thaw overnight, depending on the thickness. Thawing fish at room temperature can lead to bacteria growth because the outside of the fish gets warm and begins to spoil while the center is still frozen. If you need to thaw fish quickly, submerge the unopened package in a bowl of cold water until thawed. Depending on the amount of fish you are thawing, this could take one to two hours. Use thawed fish within twenty-four hours.

BASIC PREPARATION TECHNIQUES

Although specific preparation directions are given in each recipe, the basics, such as scaling, removing the gills, filleting, skinning, removing pin bones, and skin-drying salmon, are detailed here. If you ask, a fishmonger will usually do some of these tasks for you. As a courtesy, I prefer to call in advance and place an order. That way, rather than me walking into the shop at a busy time, the fishmonger has time to prepare my fish without rushing.

SCALING A FISH

All the recipes in this book specify in the ingredients list whether the salmon needs to be scaled or not. Scaling salmon is necessary if you are planning to cook a whole fish, fillets, or steaks with the skin on. This is a messy job, and, honestly, not a favorite of mine, so if you are buying fish that needs to be scaled, ask the fishmonger to do it for you. If you find that you must do it yourself, here's how.

If working with a whole fish, spread several layers of newspaper in the sink, covering it well, and place the fish on top. You can also place the fish in a very large plastic bag to contain the scales as they come flying off. Using kitchen shears, cut off the three fins on the underbelly, then turn the fish over and remove the dorsal fins if they are still attached. Using a fish scaler (available at cookware stores) or the back of a rigid knife blade (I use a small chef's knife), scrape the skin from the tail toward the head. Run your hands over the fish to feel for any scales you've missed. Rinse off the fish and pat dry with paper towels.

If you are working with portioned fillets, place the salmon flesh-side down on a clean cutting board. Using a fish scaler or the back of a rigid knife blade, gently scrape the scales "against the grain," so they lift and release from the skin. I do this very slowly to avoid pulling and damaging the cut flesh. I also wipe off the knife blade frequently with a folded dry paper towel to remove the scales as I work. Rinse off the fillets and pat dry with clean paper towels.

REMOVING THE GILLS

Salmon breathe through their gills, feathery tissues that allow the fish to extract oxygen from the water in exchange for carbon dioxide. The gills need to be removed if you are cooking a whole salmon, or if you are using the head to make salmon stock, because they contain impurities and will make a sauce or stock taste bitter. Lift up the gill plate—the flap just behind the eyes—on one side of the head and you'll see the gills, which are pink or red, crescent shaped, and attached at the head and at the collarbone. Using sharp kitchen shears or a knife, cut out the gills on one side of the head at the two attached points. Turn the fish over and repeat to remove the gills from the other side. Discard the gills, rinse the fish, and pat it dry with paper towels.

FILLETING A FISH

If you are purchasing a whole salmon and are planning to fillet it, ask the fishmonger to fillet it for you. It takes a little practice to get clean, smooth fillets off the bones without jagged cuts. But if you want to fillet the fish yourself, here is the method I use. Assuming the salmon has already been cleaned through the belly (see Cleaning and Gutting a Whole Salmon, page 31), place the salmon on its side and make a diagonal cut just behind the gill cover. Do this on both sides and then cut through

to detach the head. Using a sharp, flexible boning knife, slice down the length of the fish, starting at the head end and cutting all the way through the spine bone. Again, starting at the head end and working your way down to the tail while keeping your knife almost flat against the bones, skim the knife along the bones in a smooth sliding motion, trying not to stop. As you slice, lift the fillet with your other hand, which will allow you to see the flesh being sliced away from the bone. Slice in this manner all the way down to the tail. Turn the salmon over and repeat the process on the other side to remove the second fillet. Trim off the rib bones from the upper side of each fillet. If desired, save the head, bones, and trimmings for making salmon stock.

SKINNING A FILLET

Lay the salmon fillet skin-side down and with the tail facing you. With your non-dominant hand, grip the tail with a piece of paper towel, or put a little coarse salt on your fingertips to create traction. Using a sharp, flexible boning knife in your dominant hand, angle the blade toward the skin and, while continuing to grip the tail skin securely, cut along the skin as smoothly as you can. Cut all the way from the tail to the head end, keeping the skin taut. Discard the skin.

REMOVING THE PIN BONES

Run your fingertips along the flesh side of the fillet until you feel the pin bones. To remove a pin bone, using either clean needle-nose pliers (I keep a pair in the kitchen precisely for this use) or fish tweezers, grasp the end of each bone and pull it straight out and away from you. If you try to pull the bones upward or backward, the flesh will tear.

PORTIONING FILLETS

Most of the main-course recipes in this book call for a 6-oz [170-g] salmon fillet as a portion size. Although restaurants sometimes serve as much as 8 oz [230 g] for a main course, I think it is an unnecessarily large serving. In addition, most of the recipes call for fillet portions rather than steaks. Salmon steaks, unless they are cut from the tail end, are tricky to cook because the belly flaps (the thin pieces at the ends of the steaks) hang down and cook more quickly than the center of the steak. You can bone salmon steaks and tie them into medallions, but this is a fussy and time-consuming job.

There are several ways to cut salmon fillets from a boned side of salmon. To create straight-sided fillets, place a whole fillet skin-side up and cut the fillet crosswise into straight-sided portions. Or, cut the fillet in half lengthwise and then cut the halves crosswise into portions. If you want to serve only the thicker portions, reserve the belly portion for chowder or tartare. To create diagonally sliced fillets, start at the head end and follow the natural diagonal line of the fillet. Cut fillet portions on a sharp angle through the flesh. If you look at the cross section of the portion, it should be a parallelogram with angled sides rather than a rectangle. As you cut portions, you will need to make the pieces at the head end narrower than those at the tail end to achieve the same weight per serving. Finally, to achieve a butterfly cut from a skinless square-cut portion of salmon, cut straight down the middle of the flesh but not all the way through. Fold back the halves as if the piece of salmon were a butterfly opening its wings. It should look like a salmon steak without the bone in the center. Make a slightly deeper cut if the butterflied portion will not lie flat.

SKIN-DRYING SALMON

Over the years, I have learned many tips and techniques from chefs who focus on fish, such as Eric Ripert of Le Bernardin and Rick Moonen of RM Seafood. The technique of skin-drying salmon discussed here was explained in exacting detail by Thomas Keller, owner of the famed French Laundry restaurant in Yountville, California, and Per Se in New York City, in an article that appeared a number of years ago in the *Los Angeles Times*. Keller wrote, "The skin of many fish is exquisite, never more so than when it's crisped to a delicate wafer-thin crunch accompanying the sweet, soft flesh. Crisp fish skin should taste clean and fresh, with the concentrated flavor of the fish itself. Its colors and design are vivid on the plate. The fork clicks on its surface. It cracks brittlely beneath a knife."

The secret is to remove as much water as possible from the skin of the fish before you cook it. Keller continued, "Remove some of that water mechanically, by drawing a knife blade firmly back and forth over the fish, the way a wiper blade moves across a windshield. The pressure compresses the skin and squeezes the water to the surface, and the knife blade carries it away. Repeat this until no more water rises to the surface." Periodically wipe the knife blade clean with a paper towel to remove what looks like grayish scum.

BRINING

I have brined turkeys and chickens, and I have brined pork, all with great success to improve the tenderness, flavor, and moistness of the meat. And now, in the course of developing and researching recipe ideas for this book, I have brined fish with the same terrific results. Brining salmon before cooking helps inhibit the secretion of albumen, the white protein between muscle fibers that leaches out during cooking. Here are the simple directions.

SIMPLE BRINE

Makes 4 cups [960 ml]

¼ cup [30 g] flake sea salt, such as Maldon

4 cups [960 ml] ice-cold water

Four to six 6-oz [170-g] salmon fillets

1 Combine the salt and water in a container large enough to hold the fish and liquid. (I often use a 2-qt/2-L glass measure.) Stir to dissolve the salt. Add the salmon and set aside for 20 minutes.

2 Remove the salmon from the brine and rinse briefly under cold running water. Pat the salmon dry and it is ready to cook. (You can brine the fish up to 8 hours in advance and refrigerate it until you are ready to prepare the recipe.)

Note: You can add herbs, spices, and other aromatics to the brine, if you desire.

CHAPTER 3:
RAW AND CURED

Am I a risk taker when it comes to eating? I am no Anthony Bourdain, or Andrew Zimmern of the Travel Channel's *Bizarre Foods*. That said, on plenty of occasions I do eat foods that are below the FDA's guidelines for the time and temperature required to pasteurize salmonella. I love a juicy medium-rare burger, say "yes" to soft-cooked eggs, prepare home-made mayonnaise with a raw egg, and eat cheese made with raw milk.

Although salmonella bacteria are not a concern when consuming sea-food, certain parasites are. This applies to eating salmon raw or cured, the technique explored in this chapter. It also applies to eating salmon below the FDA's recommended temperature for cooking fish to 145°F [63°C]. In my opinion, and in the opinion of most chefs I know, cooking fish to that high a temperature ruins its texture and moistness. I like my fish cooked medium-rare, between 115° and 120°F [45° and 49°C], and here I am, alive and well, writing an entire book about salmon.

How do I minimize the risk of parasites? I purchase fish from a res-ponsible source and handle it properly. Some fish, like tuna, farmed salmon, swordfish, and other freshwater fish, are considered safe to eat raw or cooked to medium or medium-rare. Other fish, including wild salmon, may have parasites that are naturally occurring and not the result of contamination. (After all, insects are in fruits and vegetables.) Roundworms (*anisakid nematodes*) and the larvae of tapeworms (*Diphyllobothrium spp.*) are the most common parasites found in fish.

When preparing and consuming raw salmon (tartare, carpaccio, sashimi, or sushi) or lightly preserved salmon (ceviche, pickled, or gravlax), use commercially frozen or flash-frozen fish that has been stored at -35°F [-37°C] or below for a minimum of fifteen hours. This kills the parasites.

Now, let's get on to preparing the fabulous recipes in this chapter for tartare, ceviche, carpaccio, and gravlax.

SALMON
CARPACCIO WITH CELERY ROOT SLAW

Serves 6 as a first course

I like to pair salmon and celery root because they complement each other in texture and taste. In this dish, silky, wafer-thin slices of lightly cured salmon contrast beautifully with the matchstick-cut crunch of the raw root. The slaw is tossed in a mustardy mayonnaise-based dressing and accented with chives and parsley. Minced cornichons and capers are added to punch up the tang of the dressing and deliver textural interest. If you have time, make the slaw a day in advance of serving to allow all the flavors to meld.

CELERY ROOT SLAW

¼ cup [60 ml] mayonnaise

¼ cup [60 ml] sour cream

1½ tsp whole-grain mustard

2 tsp fresh lemon juice

1½ tsp cider vinegar

1 Tbsp minced cornichons

1 Tbsp drained brined capers, rinsed, patted dry, and minced

Fine sea salt

Freshly ground black pepper

One 1-lb [455-g] celery root

2 Tbsp finely snipped fresh chives

1 Tbsp minced fresh flat-leaf parsley

CARPACCIO

One 1-lb [455-g] center-cut salmon fillet (see Cook's Note, page 46), skin and pin bones removed

6 Tbsp [90 ml] lemon-infused extra-virgin olive oil

Flake sea salt, such as Maldon

1   TO MAKE THE SLAW: In a large bowl, whisk together the mayonnaise, sour cream, mustard, lemon juice, vinegar, cornichons, and capers. Season with fine sea salt and pepper. Set aside.

2   Using a sharp knife, cut off the base and a thin slice from the top of the celery root and then cut the root in half lengthwise. Pare away the tough outer skin from one of the halves. Using a chef's knife, mandoline, or the julienne blade of a food processor, cut the peeled half into matchsticks. Immediately add the matchsticks to the bowl holding the dressing and toss to coat them thoroughly to prevent browning. Repeat with the second half of the celery root. Add the chives and parsley and mix well. Taste and adjust the seasoning. Cover and refrigerate for at least 1 hour before serving. (This would be a good time to chill six salad plates for serving. The slaw can be prepared up to 1 day in advance and stored in a covered container in the refrigerator.)

3   TO PREPARE THE CARPACCIO: Using a very sharp, thin-bladed knife, slice the fish crosswise (against the grain) into 18 wafer-thin slices. Lay the slices side by side on a large baking sheet. Brush both sides of each salmon slice with the olive oil. Season the top side of each slice with flake sea salt. Set aside for 20 minutes.

4   Divide the salmon evenly among chilled salad plates, overlapping the slices slightly. Spoon a generous serving of the slaw next to the salmon and serve immediately.

One 8-oz [230-g] center-cut salmon fillet (see Cook's Note), skin and pin bones removed

1 Tbsp minced fresh chives, plus more for garnish

1 Tbsp minced shallots

1 Tbsp minced fresh flat-leaf parsley

1½ tsp fresh lemon juice

1 Tbsp extra-virgin olive oil, plus more for drizzling

¾ tsp fine sea salt

1 or 2 pinches of freshly ground white pepper

1 English cucumber

Flake sea salt, such as Maldon

1 Using a very sharp knife, cut the salmon into ¼-in [6-mm] dice. Place the salmon in a medium bowl. Gently fold in the chives, shallots, parsley, and lemon juice. Stir in the olive oil, then add the fine sea salt and pepper and mix gently. Cover and refrigerate for at least 30 minutes, or up to 8 hours. Remove from the refrigerator 20 minutes before serving.

2 Cut the cucumber in half crosswise. Using a sharp knife or serrated peeler, cut each half lengthwise into paper-thin slices. Set aside on a plate, covered, until ready to serve.

3 Using six large salad or dinner plates, scatter several cucumber slices around each plate in a random, artful way. Leave the center of each plate open. Spoon one-sixth of the salmon into a mound on the center of each plate. Drizzle olive oil over the cucumber slices, garnish with chives, and sprinkle with a bit of flake sea salt. Serve immediately.

COOK'S NOTE

Buy your salmon from a reputable fishmonger. The best kind of salmon to use for curing or for eating raw is salmon that has been flash frozen at sea. The freshly caught salmon is put on ice immediately and then sold to a "floating processor" vessel, where the fish is gutted and flash frozen. Any parasites in the flesh are killed when the fish is frozen solid at -35°F [-37°C] or below for a minimum of fifteen hours.

SALMON
TARTARE WITH FRESH HERBS AND CUCUMBER RIBBONS

Serves 6 as a first course

Salmon tartare is an elegant first course that takes center stage on an oversize plate with an artful flourish of paper-thin cucumber slices strewn about. A drizzle of extra-virgin olive oil, a scattering of minced chives, and a dusting of flaky sea salt make this a showstopper for a sophisticated dinner party.

1 medium ripe mango, peeled, pitted, and cut into ¼-in [6-mm] dice

1 small red bell pepper, seeded, deribbed, and cut into ¼-in [6-mm] dice

1 small jalapeño or serrano chile, stemmed, halved lengthwise, seeded, deribbed, and minced

½ cup [15 g] chopped fresh cilantro leaves

⅓ cup [45 g] finely diced red onion

2 Tbsp fresh lime juice, plus ⅓ cup [80 ml]; plus 1 lime, cut into 6 wedges

2 Tbsp extra-virgin olive oil

2 tsp fine sea salt

One 12-oz [340-g] center-cut salmon fillet (see Cook's Note, facing page), skin and pin bones removed

SALMON
CEVICHE

Serves 6 as a first course

Salmon ceviche is a festive beginning for summer entertaining or a bright palate pick-me-up as a first course for wintertime dinner parties. Here, I spoon it into stemware for a dressed-up look, but for more casual times, it can be served in a bowl with tortillas as an appetizer for eight. It calls for a few easy do-ahead steps, but it is best eaten the day it is made.

1 In a medium bowl, combine the mango, bell pepper, chile, cilantro, red onion, 2 Tbsp lime juice, olive oil, and 1 tsp of the salt. Cover and refrigerate for at least 30 minutes, or up to 8 hours.

2 Meanwhile, using a very sharp knife, cut the salmon into ¼-in [6-mm] dice. Place the salmon in a medium bowl. (At this point the salmon can be tightly covered and refrigerated for up to 4 hours.) Gently fold in the remaining ⅓ cup [80 ml] lime juice and the remaining 1 tsp salt. Cover and refrigerate to "cook" the salmon in the citrus for at least 30 minutes, or up to 1 hour.

3 When ready to serve, pour off the lime juice from the salmon. Gently fold the salmon into the mango mixture. Spoon into martini or margarita glasses and garnish each serving with a lime wedge.

LEMON OIL–CURED **SALMON**, SALMON ROE, AND SALADE RUSSE

Serves 8 as a first course

I've taken liberties with an old-fashioned main-course salad and made it an all-vegetable dish. The original luxe presentation, which the French call salade russe and included both lobster and caviar, was created in 1860 by celebrated French chef Lucien Olivier of the Hermitage restaurant in Moscow. This humble variation is composed of diced potatoes and carrots and peas that are accented with capers and bound with an herb-flecked mayonnaise dressing. The lemon oil–cured salmon served alongside the vegetables makes this cold first course fancy enough for a dinner party. Or, serve this distinctive combination as the centerpiece for a weekend brunch. The optional garnish of salmon roe ups the opulence.

SALADE RUSSE

⅔ cup [165 ml] mayonnaise

1 Tbsp Champagne or white wine vinegar

1 Tbsp finely snipped fresh chives

1 Tbsp minced fresh flat-leaf parsley

Fine sea salt

Freshly ground black pepper

2 Tbsp drained brined capers, rinsed and patted dry

5 cups [1.2 L] water

½ lemon, thinly sliced

1 bay leaf

4 peppercorns

1¼ lb [570 g] red-skinned potatoes, peeled and diced

¾ cup [105 g] peeled and diced carrots

½ cup [70 g] frozen green peas

SALMON

One 1-lb [455-g] center-cut salmon fillet (see Cook's Note, page 46), skin and pin bones removed

2 Tbsp fresh lemon juice

3 Tbsp extra-virgin olive oil

Flake sea salt, such as Maldon

Freshly ground black pepper

2 Tbsp finely snipped fresh chives

2 oz [60 g] salmon roe (optional)

1 TO MAKE THE SALADE RUSSE: In a small bowl, whisk together the mayonnaise, vinegar, chives, parsley, ¾ tsp fine sea salt, and ¼ tsp pepper. Fold in the capers. Taste and adjust the seasoning. Set aside.

2 Have ready a slotted spoon or a wire-mesh skimmer and a large bowl of ice water. In a 4-qt [3.8-L] saucepan, combine the water, lemon slices, bay leaf, peppercorns, and 1 tsp fine sea salt and bring to a boil over high heat. Adjust the heat and simmer for 10 minutes. Turn the heat to medium-low, add the potatoes, and simmer gently until the potatoes are tender but not falling apart, 8 to 10 minutes. Using the slotted spoon or skimmer, transfer the potatoes to the ice water to cool, about 2 minutes. Scoop the potatoes out of the ice water and gently blot dry with paper towels.

3 Cook the carrots until crisp-tender, scoop out, cool, and blot dry in the same way, but simmer the carrots for only 5 to 7 minutes. Repeat with the peas, simmering for about 1 minute.

Continued

4   In a medium bowl, combine the potatoes, carrots, and peas. Add the dressing and toss to coat thoroughly. Taste and adjust the seasoning. Cover the salad and refrigerate for at least 2 hours before serving to allow the flavors to meld. (The salad can be made up to 1 day in advance, covered, and refrigerated until ready to serve.) Chill eight salad plates for serving.

5   **TO PREPARE THE SALMON:** Using a very sharp, thin-bladed knife, cut the salmon in half lengthwise down the center of the fillet. Cut each half crosswise into 16 thin slices, for a total of 32 slices. Lay the slices side by side on a large plate or baking sheet. (At this point, the salmon can be sealed tightly by pressing a large sheet of plastic wrap directly onto the flesh. Smooth the plastic wrap to press out any air pockets, then refrigerate the salmon for up to 1 hour before serving.)

6   In a small bowl, whisk together the lemon juice and olive oil. Brush both sides of each salmon slice with the lemon oil. Season the top side of each slice with flake sea salt and pepper.

7   Mound a generous serving of the salad in the center of each chilled plate. Using four salmon slices per plate, arrange two slices side by side on each side of the salad. Sprinkle some of the chives over each piece of salmon and top the salad with a tiny spoonful of the salmon roe, if desired. Serve immediately.

SCANDINAVIAN-STYLE SALMON GRAVLAX

Serves 12 as a first course or 20 as an appetizer

One of the most delicate and simple salmon preparations is gravlax, a Scandinavian specialty in which the fish is cured in a salt-and-sugar rub. No cooking is involved. I like to think of these paper-thin slices of cured fish as one step beyond Japanese sashimi. Typically, gravlax is seasoned with fresh dill, a brandy such as Cognac, and spruce sprigs. Not everyone has a spruce tree growing in his or her yard, including me, so I've decided to re-create that woodsy flavor by including gin in my recipe. The mild juniper flavor of the gin is a lovely accent with the dill. Aquavit works well, too.

½ cup [100 g] coarse sea salt, such as La Baleine

½ cup [100 g] sugar

One 3- to 4-lb [1.4- to 1.8-kg] salmon fillet, skin on and pin bones removed

10 sprigs fresh dill, coarsely chopped

¼ cup [60 ml] gin or aquavit

Finely snipped fresh chives; thinly sliced green onions, including green tops; brined capers, drained, rinsed, and blotted dry; minced shallots; and/or English cucumber, thinly sliced, for garnish

Thinly sliced pumpernickel or other bread for serving

1 Select a deep glass or ceramic baking dish the same length as the fish or nearly so. In a small bowl, stir together the salt and sugar. Spread half of the salt mixture on the bottom of the baking dish. Lay the salmon, skin-side down, in the dish. Gently rub the remaining salt mixture over the flesh side of the fillet. Sprinkle the dill evenly over the fillet. Slowly drizzle the gin evenly over the top, being careful not to rinse off the salt cure.

2 Place a large sheet of plastic wrap directly on top of the fish. Rest a slightly smaller baking dish or other flat, rimmed vessel on top of the covered fish. Put something that weighs about 3 lb [1.4 kg] in the top dish. (I use full beer bottles set on their sides.) Place the weighted salmon in the refrigerator for at least 2 days, or up to 5 days. Flip the salmon once a day, being sure to return the weighted baking dish to the top of the salmon after each turn.

3 Remove the weight, the top dish, and the plastic wrap. The salt cure will be completely dissolved. I leave the chopped dill on the gravlax. (Scrape it off, if desired.) Skin the fillet and then cut crosswise (against the grain) into thin slices. Arrange the slices on a platter or overlap several slices on individual plates and garnish as desired. Serve with the pumpernickel.

COOK'S NOTE

If not serving the cured salmon right away, it can be wrapped tightly in plastic wrap and stored in the refrigerator for up to 1 week. Or, wrap it in plastic wrap and then in a double layer of aluminum foil and place in the freezer for up to 3 months. Thaw overnight in the refrigerator before serving.

½ cup [100 g] coarse sea salt, such as La Baleine

½ cup [100 g] firmly packed golden brown sugar

One 3- to 4-lb [1.4- to 1.8-kg] salmon fillet, skin on and pin bones removed

8 oz [230 g] raw beets, peeled and grated

1 cup [240 g] prepared extra-hot horseradish

¼ cup [60 ml] vodka

Finely snipped fresh chives; thinly sliced green onions, including green tops; brined capers, drained, rinsed, and blotted dry; minced shallots; and/or English cucumber, thinly sliced, for garnish

Thinly sliced pumpernickel or other bread for serving

BEET AND HORSERADISH CURED SALMON GRAVLAX

Serves 12 as a first course or 20 as an appetizer

In this variation of traditional gravlax, raw grated beets and fresh horseradish are mixed together and spread on top of the salt cure. The horseradish subtly flavors the salmon and the beets penetrate the top of the flesh, coloring the surface with a ruby glow. The result is divine in looks and taste and is simply gorgeous when sliced!

1   Select a rimmed baking sheet that is the same length as the salmon or nearly so. Place a wire rack that is just slightly shorter inside the baking sheet. Cover the rack with a double layer of cheesecloth, allowing enough to overhang the sides and ends of the rack to fold over and cover the fish completely.

2   In a small bowl, stir together the salt and brown sugar. Spread half of the salt mixture on the skin side of the salmon, packing it into place. Lay the salmon, skin-side down, on the cheesecloth. Gently rub the remaining salt mixture over the flesh side of the fillet.

3   In a medium bowl, combine the beets and horseradish and mix well. Spread the beet mixture over the top and sides of the salmon fillet. Slowly drizzle the vodka evenly over the top, being careful not to rinse off the beet-salt cure.

4   Bring up the sides of the cheesecloth and wrap them snugly around the fish. Fold the overhanging ends toward the center. Now seal the entire fillet in a large sheet of plastic wrap. Once tightly wrapped, arrange the fillet, flesh-side up, on the rack. Rest a slightly smaller rimmed baking sheet or other flat, rimmed vessel on top of the fish. Put something that weighs about 3 lb [1.4 kg] on the top baking sheet. (I use full beer bottles set on their sides.) Place the weighted salmon in the refrigerator for at least 2 days, or up to 5 days. Flip the salmon once a day, being sure to return the weighted baking sheet to the top of the salmon after each turn.

5   Remove the weighted baking sheet. Remove the fillet from the wrappings and scrape the cure off of the flesh side. Skin the fillet and then cut crosswise (against the grain) into thin slices. (To store, see Cook's Note, page 51). Arrange the slices on a platter or on individual plates and garnish as desired. Serve with the pumpernickel.

PASTRAMI SALMON

Serves 8 to 10 as part of a brunch

While researching all the different ways to cure salmon, I ran across several old recipes for salmon cured with pastrami spices. I was intrigued. I mean, how could this not be delicious? I love lox. I love beef pastrami. Pairing salmon with this bold spice blend was worthy of my time in the kitchen. I combined a couple of techniques and decided to do a short cure time at room temperature, and then finish the salmon by smoking it briefly on the stove top. You can serve this salmon as you would lox, with cream cheese (or soft goat cheese) and bagels. Or, toast some pumpernickel or rye bread, smear it with a little dark mustard, and top it with slices of the cured salmon.

PASTRAMI SPICE MIXTURE

2 Tbsp pink peppercorns

1½ Tbsp dry-packed green peppercorns

1 Tbsp black peppercorns

1½ tsp coriander seeds

2 Tbsp sweet paprika

1 Tbsp five-spice powder

½ cup [100 g] coarse sea salt, such as La Baleine

½ cup [100 g] sugar

½ cup [15 g] chopped fresh dill

One 2- to 2½-lb [910-g to 1.2-kg] center-cut salmon fillet, skin on and scaled, pin bones removed

You will also need

¼ cup [20 g] pulverized apple-wood smoking chips

1 **TO MAKE THE SPICE MIXTURE:** Combine the pink, green, and black peppercorns and the coriander seeds in small, heavy-bottomed frying pan, preferably cast iron. Place the pan over medium-low heat and toast the spices, stirring frequently, until very fragrant, about 2 minutes. Remove from the heat, transfer to a small bowl, and let cool for 5 minutes.

2 Using a mortar and pestle or a spice grinder (or a very clean coffee grinder), pulverize the toasted spices to a fine powder. Return the ground spices to the small bowl and stir in the paprika and five-spice powder. (The mixture will keep in an airtight container at room temperature for up to 3 months.)

3 In a medium bowl, combine the salt, sugar, dill, and 1½ Tbsp of the pastrami spice mixture and mix well.

4 Select a deep glass or ceramic baking dish the same length as the fish or nearly so. Spread half of the salt mixture on the skin side of the salmon. Lay the salmon, skin-side down, in the dish. Gently rub the remaining salt mixture over the flesh side of the fillet. Cover the dish with plastic wrap and set aside at room temperature for 5 hours, flipping the salmon and re-covering the dish after 2½ hours.

Continued

5 Using a stove-top smoker or a wok, line the bottom of the pan with a sheet of heavy-duty aluminum foil. (Using heavy-duty foil makes for easier cleanup.) Pour the smoking chips onto the foil in the center of the pan and spread in an even layer over the center. Sprinkle 1 Tbsp of the pastrami spice mixture evenly over the top. Drizzle a few drops of water over the spice mixture. If using a stove-top smoker, lay another piece of foil on top, covering all of the wood-smoking mixture. Cover a drip tray with foil and place it on top of the second piece of foil. If using a wok, lay a large sheet of foil loosely over the wood-smoking mixture. Coat a wire rack with nonstick cooking spray and place on top of the drip tray or the foil.

6 Scrape the salt mixture off both sides of the salmon with the back of a knife. Wipe each side of the salmon with a damp paper towel until most of the salt is removed. Arrange the salmon, flesh-side up, on the rack. Slide the lid on the stove-top smoker or cover the wok, leaving it slightly open, and then place the smoker or wok over medium heat. When the first wisp of smoke appears, close the lid or tightly cover the wok. Smoke the salmon for 5 minutes. Turn off the heat and leave the salmon in the smoker or wok, covered, for an additional 5 minutes.

7 Transfer the salmon to a plate to cool. Wrap tightly in plastic wrap and refrigerate. (Once cured and smoked, the salmon will keep in the refrigerator for up to 10 days.)

8 When ready to serve, transfer the salmon to a cutting board. Slide a spatula between the salmon flesh and the skin, separating them, and discard the skin. Cut the salmon crosswise (against the grain) into thin slices. Arrange the slices on a platter and serve.

SALMON PICKLED IN THE STYLE OF HERRING

Serves 8 as part of a brunch

Growing up in a Jewish home, Sunday brunch was a big affair. My father would take me along to do the shopping. We'd stop at the old Jewish deli for hand-sliced Nova Scotia lox, pickled herring, and smoked sablefish. Then we'd head to the greengrocer for leaf lettuce, tomatoes, and red onion. We'd pick up coffee cake at the bakery and our final stop was at Bageland for just-baked bagels and a cream cheese smear. In the meantime, my mother would set the table and have plat-ters waiting. I came to understand that my father's efficient shopping scheme was devised so that the bagels were still warm when we sat down to eat. My love for smoked and pickled fish led me to explore pickling salmon for this book. It's a new favorite, and I would have loved it as a child had I tasted it then. Sockeye salmon or the thinner tail section of a chinook, coho, or even pink salmon are my preferences for pickling.

4 cups [960 ml] water

1½ cups [375 ml] unseasoned rice vinegar

½ cup [100 g] sugar

1½ Tbsp fine sea salt

4 bay leaves, crushed

2 whole cloves

1 Tbsp coriander seeds

1 Tbsp dill seeds

1 Tbsp yellow mustard seeds

1½ tsp black peppercorns

1 tsp whole allspice

One 2-lb [910-g] salmon fillet, skin and pin bones removed, cut into 1½-in [4-cm] squares

1 white onion, halved and thinly sliced

1 In a medium saucepan, combine the water, vinegar, sugar, and salt and bring to a boil over high heat, stirring frequently to dissolve the sugar and salt. Remove from the heat and let cool completely.

2 Meanwhile, in a small bowl, combine the bay leaves, cloves, coriander seeds, dill seeds, mustard seeds, peppercorns, and allspice and mix well. Set aside.

3 In a ceramic crock or glass container with a tight-fitting lid, arrange a single layer of salmon, sprinkle some of the spice mixture on top, and then add a layer of onion. Continue to add layers in this order until you have used up all the salmon, spice mixture, and onion, ending with the onion. Pour the cooled brine mixture over the top. Press down on the contents of the container so all the solids are immersed in the brine. Cover and refrigerate for at least 4 days, or up to 10 days.

4 Serve the salmon along with the pickled onions.

CHAPTER 4:
ON THE
STOVE TOP

Some of my favorite salmon-cooking techniques—smoking, poaching, braising, pan searing, and stir-frying—can be mastered on the stove top. You can invest in a fish poacher if you like, but it isn't necessary. I find my large, straight-sided sauté pan with a tight-fitting lid works fabulously for the Wine-Poached Salmon Steaks on page 63. I use the same pan for braising and make two easy weeknight favorites, Shanghai-Style Poached Salmon (page 65) and Green Curry Braised Salmon (page 66). Both of these dishes also make great dinner-party fare.

A well-seasoned cast-iron frying pan, the workhorse pan every cook should own, will have you pan searing like a pro. Use it to cook Crisp Rice-Coated Salmon with a Citrus Sriracha Sauce (page 69) or Crispy-Skin Pan-Seared Salmon with Summertime Succotash (page 74) and achieve restaurant-quality results.

Salmon is exquisite when tea-smoked in a wok (see page 60) or alder-smoked in a stove-top smoker (see page 62). Stir-frying, a cooking method I have used for many years, was not a technique I considered for salmon. I thought the delicate flesh of the fish would fall apart into flakes, until my colleague and friend Grace Young generously shared her method for stir-frying salmon. You'll find the recipe for Salmon Stir-Fry with Snow Peas and Shiitake Mushrooms on page 77.

No place to grill outside? With a stove-top grill pan and a kitchen with good ventilation, you can grill indoors. This is an especially handy technique for apartment dwellers. Check out the quick-to-assemble Indian Spice–Rubbed Pan-Grilled Salmon on page 68. You can also easily adapt the recipe for salmon skewers on page 124 to a stove-top grill pan.

One 1½-lb [680-g] center-cut salmon fillet, skin on and scaled, pin bones removed

¼ cup [20 g] Earl Grey, oolong, or Lapsang souchong whole-leaf tea

¼ cup [50 g] firmly packed golden brown sugar

¼ cup [50 g] uncooked white rice

Fine sea salt

Freshly ground black pepper

TEA-SMOKED SALMON

Serves 6

Once you have made tea-smoked salmon, whether in a stove-top smoker, a wok, or on the grill, you'll wonder how a piece of fish with almost no embellishments can taste so good. Serve the salmon on a bed of jasmine rice with stir-fried sugar snap peas or steamed baby bok choy.

1 Remove the salmon from the refrigerator 30 minutes before smoking to bring it to room temperature.

2 In a small bowl, combine the tea leaves, brown sugar, and rice and mix well. Set aside.

3 Using a stove-top smoker or a wok, line the bottom of the pan with a sheet of heavy-duty aluminum foil. (Using heavy-duty foil makes for easier cleanup.) Pour the tea-rice mixture onto the foil in the center of the pan and spread in an even layer over the center. If using a stove-top smoker, lay another piece of foil on top, covering all of the tea-rice mixture. Cover a drip tray with foil and place it on top of the second piece of foil. If using a wok, lay a large sheet of foil loosely over the tea-rice mixture. Coat a wire rack with nonstick cooking spray and place on top of the drip tray or foil.

4 Arrange the salmon on the rack and sprinkle with salt and pepper. Slide the lid on the stove-top smoker or cover the wok, leaving it slightly open, and then place the smoker or wok over medium heat. When the first wisp of smoke appears, close the lid or tightly cover the wok. Smoke the salmon for 15 to 17 minutes. Turn off the heat and leave the salmon in the smoker, covered, for an additional 5 minutes.

5 Transfer the salmon to a cutting board. Slide a spatula between the salmon flesh and the skin, separating them, and discard the skin. Cut the salmon crosswise (against the grain) into six portions. Serve immediately.

One 1½-lb [680-g] center-cut salmon fillet, skin on and scaled, pin bones removed

½ lemon

Fine sea salt

Freshly ground black pepper

You will also need

Heaping 1 Tbsp pulverized alder-wood smoking chips

STOVE-TOP ALDER-SMOKED SALMON

Serves 6

Delicious all by itself, this aromatic smoked salmon can be sliced and served as part of a brunch or dinner menu. Or, you can assemble a salad while the salmon is smoking, add the salmon once it is done, and then offer the result as a big-flavored main course. Consider a smoked-salmon Caesar salad, or use mildly bitter, frizzy greens, such as curly endive; add chopped bacon and hard-cooked eggs; and then toss everything in a creamy vinaigrette. In the summer, I like to make a composed salad with radishes, tomatoes, avocado, and baby red potatoes. Leftover smoked salmon is ideal in sandwiches, flaked into a pasta dish, or cut into small chunks and added to chowder.

1 Remove the salmon from the refrigerator 30 minutes before smoking to bring it to room temperature.

2 Using a stove-top smoker or a wok, line the bottom of the pan with a sheet of heavy-duty aluminum foil. (Using heavy-duty foil makes for easier cleanup.) Place the wood chips in a small pile on the foil in the center of the pan. If using a stove-top smoker, lay another piece of foil on top, covering all of the wood chips. Cover a drip tray with foil and place it on top of the second piece of foil. If using a wok, lay a large sheet of foil loosely over the wood chips. Coat a wire rack with nonstick cooking spray and place on top of the drip tray or foil.

3 Arrange the salmon on the rack, squeeze the juice from the lemon half over the salmon, and sprinkle lightly with salt and pepper. Slide the lid on the stove-top smoker or cover the wok, leaving it slightly open, and then place the smoker or wok over medium heat. When the first wisp of smoke appears, close the lid or tightly cover the wok. Smoke the salmon for 15 to 17 minutes. Turn off the heat and leave the salmon in the smoker, covered, for an additional 5 minutes.

4 Transfer the salmon to a cutting board. Slide a spatula between the salmon flesh and the skin, separating them, and discard the skin. Cut the salmon crosswise (against the grain) into six portions. Serve immediately.

4 thick-cut salmon steaks, about 6 oz [170 g] each, skin and pin bones removed

2 cups [480 ml] dry Riesling

½ cup [120 ml] water

2 star anise pods

10 peppercorns

1 Tbsp extra-virgin olive oil

2 Tbsp chopped fresh cilantro leaves

Fine sea salt

Freshly ground black pepper

WINE-POACHED SALMON STEAKS

Serves 4

A dieter's delight! Nothing could be simpler and tastier than a glorious fresh salmon fillet poached in wine. Riesling is my go-to varietal for poaching fish. I add the subtle spicing of star anise and peppercorns, which imparts a bit of exotic flavor, but it's the rich full taste of the salmon that makes this main course special. It is perfect for either an easy weeknight meal or a dinner for company. Serve the salmon with steamed asparagus, green beans, or sugar snap peas.

1 Remove the salmon from the refrigerator 30 minutes before cooking to bring it to room temperature.

2 In a sauté pan just large enough to hold the salmon steaks in a single layer, combine the wine, water, star anise, and peppercorns. Bring to a boil over medium heat, turn the heat to low, and simmer for 5 minutes. Using a spatula, carefully slip the salmon into the pan. (The salmon should be completely submerged in the poaching liquid. If it isn't, add a bit more water.) Cover the pan and poach the salmon until almost opaque throughout, or an instant-read thermometer inserted into the center registers 125°F [52°C] or a little above, about 8 minutes.

3 Transfer the salmon to warmed dinner plates or shallow pasta bowls. Drizzle each fillet with a little of the olive oil and sprinkle the cilantro on top. Taste the poaching liquid and season lightly with salt and pepper. Spoon 2 to 3 Tbsp of the poaching liquid around each fillet. Serve immediately.

4 salmon fillets, about 6 oz [170 g] each, skin and pin bones removed

SWEET VINEGAR SAUCE

½ cup [120 ml] soy sauce

¼ cup [60 ml] distilled white vinegar

¼ cup [50 g] sugar

4 green onions, including green tops, cut into 1-in [2.5-cm] lengths

4 thin slices fresh ginger, peeled and julienned

3 cups [720 ml] water

3 green onions, including green tops, cut into 1-in [2.5-cm] lengths

5 thin slices fresh ginger, peeled

SHANGHAI-STYLE POACHED SALMON

Serves 4

Here, I am taking liberties with a classic Shanghai-style braised whole fish by using salmon fillet cut into individual portions. The salmon is first cooked in water that has been simmered with ginger and green onions. Before it is fully cooked, almost all the liquid is drained off and the fish is basted in a sweet vinegar sauce and cooked through. I like to serve this dish with steamed jasmine rice, spooning some of the sauce over the rice.

1 Remove the salmon from the refrigerator 30 minutes before cooking to bring it to room temperature.

2 **TO MAKE THE SAUCE:** In a small bowl, stir together the soy sauce, vinegar, and sugar until the sugar is dissolved. Stir in the 4 green onions and julienned ginger. Set aside.

3 In a sauté pan just large enough to hold the salmon fillets in a single layer, combine the water, 3 green onions, and sliced ginger. Bring to a boil over medium heat, turn the heat to medium-low, and simmer for 5 minutes. Using a spatula, carefully slip the salmon into the pan. (The salmon should be completely submerged in the poaching liquid. If it isn't, add a bit more water.) Cover the pan and poach the salmon for 5 minutes.

4 Again using the spatula, lift the salmon to a plate. Carefully drain off almost all the poaching liquid from the pan, leaving only ¼ cup [60 ml] in the pan. Remove and discard the green onions and ginger from the pan. Return the pan to medium-low heat and add the vinegar sauce. Bring to a simmer, stirring occasionally. Slip the salmon back into the pan and baste with the sauce. Continue to braise the salmon, basting frequently, until almost opaque throughout, or an instant-read thermometer inserted into the center registers 125°F [52°C] or a little above, about 8 minutes. The sauce will have reduced and thickened a little.

5 Transfer the salmon to warmed dinner plates or shallow pasta bowls. Spoon the sauce around the fillets, dividing it evenly. Serve immediately.

GREEN CURRY BRAISED **SALMON**

Serves 4

While making curry paste from scratch is something I might do as a fun weekend cooking project, I also keep prepared green curry paste on hand in my refrigerator for quick-fix meals. (I like either Thai Kitchen brand, which I can find in my supermarket, or Mae Ploy brand, which is available in most Asian markets.) Without a lot of fuss, this big-flavored one-bowl meal comes together in about a half hour, making it ideal for a weeknight dinner. Accompany the salmon and snow peas with steamed jasmine rice.

4 salmon fillets, about 6 oz [170 g] each, skin and pin bones removed

One 13½-oz [405-ml] can unsweetened coconut milk

¼ cup [60 ml] Thai green curry paste

1 Tbsp firmly packed golden brown sugar

1 cup [240 ml] water

1 Tbsp Asian fish sauce, preferably Vietnamese nuoc mam

2 cups [130 g] snow peas, stem ends trimmed and strings removed

1 Tbsp fresh lime juice

3 green onions, including green tops, thinly sliced

½ cup [15 g] chopped fresh cilantro

1 Remove the salmon from the refrigerator 30 minutes before cooking to bring it to room temperature.

2 Open the can of coconut milk without first shaking it. Spoon out the thick cream that has separated and risen to the top. Set the cream aside in a small bowl. Pour off the remaining thin coconut milk and reserve it separately.

3 In a large sauté pan, warm the coconut cream over medium-low heat. Add the curry paste and whisk until the mixture is smooth and comes to a simmer. Add the brown sugar and stir until dissolved. Add the thin coconut milk, water, and fish sauce and bring to a simmer, stirring once or twice. Add the salmon fillets in a single layer, turn the heat to low, cover, and simmer for 5 minutes. Flip the salmon, re-cover, and cook for 2 minutes longer. Scatter the snow peas around the salmon, submerging them in the liquid, re-cover the pan, and cook until the snow peas are bright green and the salmon is cooked through, about 2 minutes longer. Remove the pan from the heat.

4 Transfer the salmon to warmed dinner plates or shallow pasta bowls. Stir the lime juice, green onions, and cilantro into the curry sauce. Spoon the curry sauce and snow peas around the fillets, dividing the sauce and peas evenly. Serve immediately.

INDIAN SPICE–RUBBED PAN-GRILLED SALMON

Serves 4

I'll admit that I'm a wimp when it comes to grilling outside on a cold or rainy day. My husband, on the other hand, will throw on his hooded jacket—or even hold an umbrella—and fire up the grill. My easy (and warm) alternative is pan grilling indoors using a ridged, cast-iron grill pan. Even a well-seasoned cast-iron frying pan will work for this preparation. Although you won't have the telltale grill marks, you'll achieve crisp skin and a lovely thin crust on the flesh. Serve the salmon accompanied with potatoes, basmati rice, or a hearty grain such as farro or quinoa.

½ cup [120 ml] extra-virgin olive oil

2 garlic cloves, thinly sliced

1½ tsp Madras curry powder

4 center-cut salmon fillets, about 6 oz [170 g] each, skin and pin bones removed

Fine sea salt

1 In a small saucepan, stir together the olive oil, garlic, and curry powder. Warm over medium heat until fragrant and hot but not simmering. Remove from the heat and let cool to room temperature.

2 Place the salmon in a freezer-strength lock-top plastic bag. Pour the cooled oil mixture all around the fillets and rub gently to coat the salmon evenly. Press to remove any air from the bag and seal it tightly. Refrigerate the salmon for at least 8 hours, or up to overnight. Remove from the refrigerator 1 hour before cooking.

3 Remove the salmon from the plastic bag and drain off the excess oil mixture but don't blot dry. Discard the garlic slices. Set the salmon on a plate and season with salt. Heat a large grill pan, preferably cast iron, over medium-high heat. Oil the pan, then add the salmon, skin-side up, and sear on one side until beautiful grill marks are etched across the fillets, 3 to 4 minutes. Turn the fillets, skin-side down, and cook until the salmon is almost opaque throughout but still very moist, or an instant-read thermometer inserted into the center registers 115° to 120°F [45° to 49°C], about 3 minutes longer.

4 Transfer the salmon to warmed dinner plates. Serve immediately.

CRISP RICE-COATED SALMON WITH A CITRUS SRIRACHA SAUCE

Serves 4

Salmon coated with rice flakes and then browned to crisp perfection is something I ate years ago when four-star chef Gray Kunz was at the top of his game on the New York City dining scene. I don't know why, but I never bothered to translate the technique to the home kitchen until now. Rice flakes, also called flattened rice or beaten rice, are rice kernels that have been husked and then roasted and flattened to create flat, light flakes. In India, Nepal, and Bangladesh, they are a popular ingredient for fried snacks or, with coconut milk added, turned into a quick porridge. Easier to find than I suspected, I bought rice flakes at an Indian market, later saw them at a well-stocked Asian market, and even found an organic product online. As tempting as it might be to substitute Rice Krispies cereal, it will not deliver the same results.

4 center-cut salmon fillets, about 6 oz [170 g] each, skin on and scaled, pin bones removed

CITRUS SRIRACHA SAUCE

½ cup [120 ml] mayonnaise

¼ cup [60 ml] sour cream

⅓ cup [80 ml] fresh orange juice

2 tsp Sriracha (see Cook's Note)

1½ tsp unseasoned rice vinegar

1 tsp sugar

½ tsp fine sea salt

½ tsp Asian sesame oil

1 cup [50 g] rice flakes

1 egg yolk

1 tsp water

¼ tsp freshly ground black pepper

⅛ tsp cayenne pepper

Fine sea salt

3 Tbsp extra-virgin olive oil

1 Tbsp unsalted butter

Fresh cilantro sprigs for garnish

1. Remove the salmon from the refrigerator 30 minutes before cooking to bring it to room temperature. Pat dry with paper towels.

2. **TO MAKE THE SAUCE:** In a small bowl, whisk together the mayonnaise, sour cream, orange juice, Sriracha, vinegar, sugar, salt, and sesame oil until thoroughly combined. Cover and set aside until ready to serve. (The sauce can be made up to 1 day in advance, covered, and refrigerated. Remove from the refrigerator 45 minutes before serving.)

3. Spread the rice flakes in a pie plate or a wide, shallow bowl. In a small bowl, whisk together the egg yolk and water. Add the black pepper and cayenne and whisk until well mixed.

4. Season both sides of each salmon fillet with salt. Using a pastry brush, generously coat the skin side of each fillet with the egg mixture. One at a time, press the egg-coated side of each fillet into the rice flakes. If you see any holes in the coating, sprinkle more rice flakes on top and press to adhere the coating. As the fillets are coated, set them aside, coated-side up, on a plate.

Continued

5 Place a large frying pan, preferably cast iron, over medium heat. When the pan is hot, add the olive oil and swirl to coat the bottom of the pan. Add the salmon fillets, coated-side down, and cook, without disturbing, until the crusts are crisp and deeply golden brown, 4 to 5 minutes. Add the butter to the pan and swirl it around the fillets. Turn the fillets, coated-side up, and cook until the salmon is almost opaque throughout but still very moist, or an instant-read thermometer inserted into the center registers 115° to 120°F [45° to 49°C], about 3 minutes longer.

6 Place a salmon fillet, crust-side up, on each warmed dinner plate, drizzle with a generous spoonful of the sauce, and garnish with a couple of cilantro sprigs. Serve immediately.

COOK'S NOTE

Sriracha, a hot sauce made from sun-dried chiles, vinegar, garlic, sugar, and salt, is named after a port city on the Bay of Bangkok in southern Thailand. In the United States, it has been popularized by Huy Fong Foods, which packages it in a tall, clear plastic bottle with a bright green squirt top and a white rooster on the label. It is widely available in Asian markets and in supermarkets with an Asian food section. Once it has been opened, store it in the refrigerator; it will keep indefinitely.

4 center-cut salmon fillets, about 6 oz [170 g] each, skin on and scaled, pin bones removed, skin-dried (see page 40)

GREMOLATA

2 Tbsp finely chopped fresh dill

1 Tbsp finely chopped fresh flat-leaf parsley

1 garlic clove, minced

1 tsp grated lemon zest

Big pinch of fine sea salt

Small pinch of freshly ground black pepper

1 lb [455 g] baby new white potatoes

Fine sea salt

4 Tbsp [60 ml] grapeseed or other neutral oil

Freshly ground black pepper

⅓ cup [40 g] Wondra flour (see Cook's Note, page 76)

4 Tbsp [55 g] unsalted butter

1½ Tbsp fresh lemon juice

BROWN BUTTER–SEARED SALMON WITH SMASHED NEW POTATOES

Serves 4

Dinner-party worthy and pretty on the plate, a glistening crisp-skinned fillet of salmon sits atop smashed and fried new potatoes. The salmon and potatoes are surrounded by a lemon-spiked brown butter pan sauce and topped with a heady dill-parsley gremolata. If you are entertaining, make the gremolata and simmer and smash the potatoes earlier in the day to simplify the last-minute steps.

1 Remove the salmon from the refrigerator 30 minutes before cooking to bring it to room temperature.

2 **TO MAKE THE GREMOLATA:** In a small bowl, combine the dill, parsley, garlic, lemon zest, salt, and pepper and mix well. Set aside.

3 Put the potatoes in a medium pot and add water to cover by at least 1 in [2.5 cm]. Add 2 tsp salt, place over high heat, and bring to a boil. Lower the heat so the water just simmers, cover partially, and cook the potatoes until very tender when pierced with a fork, about 15 minutes.

4 Drain the potatoes in a colander and let stand until just cool enough to handle, about 10 minutes. Working with one potato at a time, place it in the palm of one hand and press gently with your other palm to flatten, forming a patty about ½ in [12 mm] thick. (The edges will split and that is fine.) As the potatoes are flattened, set them aside on a plate.

5 In a 12-in [30.5-cm] heavy frying pan, preferably cast iron, warm 2 Tbsp of the grapeseed oil over medium-high heat until hot and swirl to coat the bottom of the pan. Add the potatoes in a single layer. Fry on one side until golden brown, about 3 minutes. Turn and brown the second side, about 3 minutes longer. Transfer the potatoes to a warmed plate, sprinkle with a little salt, and keep warm. Wipe the pan clean.

6 Blot the salmon dry with paper towels. Season both sides of each salmon fillet with salt and pepper. Spread the flour in a pie plate or a wide, shallow bowl. Dip the skin side of each fillet in the flour, shaking off the excess. As the fillets are coated, set them aside, coated-side up, on a plate.

7 Return the pan to medium-high heat. Add the remaining 2 Tbsp grapeseed oil and swirl to coat the bottom of the pan. When the oil is hot but not smoking, add the salmon fillets, skin-side down, then press down on each fillet with the back of a metal spatula to maximize the contact with the surface of the pan. (This helps crisp the skin.) Cook on one side, without disturbing, until the skin is golden and crisp, about 3 minutes. Add the butter to the pan and swirl it around the fillets. Turn the fillets skin-side up and cook, basting frequently with the butter, until the salmon is almost opaque throughout but still very moist, or an instant-read thermometer inserted into the center registers 115° to 120°F [45° to 49°C], about 3 minutes longer. Transfer the salmon to a warmed plate.

8 Add the lemon juice to the pan along with ¼ tsp salt and stir to combine. Bring the sauce to a simmer and then remove from the heat.

9 Divide the potatoes evenly among warmed dinner plates, arranging them in the center of each plate. Place a salmon fillet, skin-side up, on top of each bed of potatoes and evenly spoon the brown butter sauce over the salmon and the potatoes. Sprinkle the gremolata over the salmon, dividing it evenly. Serve immediately.

CRISPY-SKIN PAN-SEARED SALMON WITH SUMMERTIME SUCCOTASH

Serves 4

Salmon and succotash are a winning combination of texture, color, and flavor. Variations abound based on the season. In late spring, when fresh wild salmon is in the market, I make succotash with corn, edamame instead of lima beans, asparagus, spring onions, and green garlic. In late summer, I might add cherry tomatoes and definitely use basil in place of parsley. In early fall, I add chanterelle mushrooms and a little fresh thyme. Note my use of Wondra flour, which adds crispness and good color to the skin and is a much better choice than all-purpose flour.

4 center-cut salmon fillets, about 6 oz [170 g] each, skin on and scaled, pin bones removed, skin-dried (see page 40)

Fine sea salt

Freshly ground black pepper

⅓ cup [40 g] Wondra flour (see Cook's Note)

2 Tbsp unsalted butter

4 Tbsp [60 ml] extra-virgin olive oil

1 large shallot, chopped

1 garlic clove, minced

1½ cups [190 g] fresh corn kernels

2 medium zucchini, cut into ½-in [12-mm] dice

1 medium red bell pepper, seeded, deribbed, and cut into ½-in [12-mm] dice

¼ cup [7 g] minced fresh basil or flat-leaf parsley

1 Remove the salmon from the refrigerator 30 minutes before cooking to bring it to room temperature. Pat dry with paper towels.

2 Season both sides of each salmon fillet with salt and pepper. Spread the flour in a pie plate or a wide, shallow bowl. Dip the skin side of each fillet in the flour, shaking off the excess. As the fillets are coated, set them aside, coated-side up, on a plate.

3 Place a large frying pan, preferably nonstick, over medium-high heat. When the pan is hot, add 1 Tbsp each of the butter and olive oil and swirl to coat the bottom of the pan. Add the shallot and garlic and sauté just until fragrant, about 1 minute. Add the corn, zucchini, and bell pepper and sauté, stirring frequently, until crisp-tender and just beginning to brown at the edges, about 5 minutes. Stir in half of the basil and season with salt and pepper. Keep the succotash warm until ready to serve.

4 Place a large frying pan, preferably cast iron, over medium-high heat. When the pan is hot, add the remaining 3 Tbsp olive oil and swirl to coat the bottom of the pan. Add the salmon fillets, skin-side down, then press down on each fillet with the back of a metal spatula to maximize the contact with the surface of the pan. (This helps crisp the skin.) Cook on one side, without disturbing, until the skin is crisp and browned, about 4 minutes. Add the remaining 1 Tbsp butter to the pan and swirl it around the fillets. Turn the fillets skin-side up and cook until the salmon is almost opaque throughout but still very moist, or an instant-read thermometer inserted into the center registers 115° to 120°F [45° to 49°C], about 3 minutes longer.

Continued

5 Spoon a generous serving of the warm succotash in the center of each warmed dinner plate, place a salmon fillet, skin-side up, on top, and garnish with the remaining basil. Serve immediately.

COOK'S NOTE

I learned from a chef friend that Wondra flour, a finely ground instant flour, is a much better choice than all-purpose flour for coating the skin of fish. In a restaurant, when a salmon fillet is served skin-side up and the skin is crackly crisp and beautifully browned, the quality of that texture and coloration comes from the coating—and Wondra flour is the secret. White rice flour is a good gluten-free option.

8 dried shiitake mushrooms

MARINADE

1 Tbsp cornstarch

1 Tbsp peanut or grapeseed oil

1 Tbsp minced garlic

1½ tsp Chinese rice wine or pale dry sherry

½ tsp Asian sesame oil

½ tsp fine sea salt

¼ tsp freshly ground black pepper

1 egg white, lightly beaten

One 1¼-lb [570-g] salmon fillet, skin and pin bones removed

5 Tbsp [75 ml] canned low-sodium chicken broth

1 Tbsp Chinese rice wine or pale dry sherry

1½ tsp Asian sesame oil

3 Tbsp peanut or grapeseed oil

2 green onions, including green tops, halved lengthwise and finely chopped

1 Tbsp peeled and finely minced fresh ginger

4 oz [115 g] snow peas, stem ends trimmed and strings removed

1 lemon, cut into wedges

SALMON STIR-FRY WITH SNOW PEAS AND SHIITAKE MUSHROOMS

Serves 4

I had never even considered stir-frying salmon until I read *Stir-Frying to the Sky's Edge*, my friend Grace Young's masterful cookbook. Her technique doesn't involve tossing the salmon about like you would when stir-frying sturdy seafood, such as shrimp or squid. Salmon is delicate and will fall apart without a clever method for cooking it. I've mimicked her approach, first marinating the salmon to coat and flavor it, and then carefully arranging the salmon in a single layer in the wok, allowing one side to brown and then braise in a sauce before turning it. Vary the vegetables if you like. Baby bok choy or parboiled asparagus instead of snow peas would work well, too.

1   In a small bowl or other small container, soak the mushrooms in hot water to cover until softened, about 20 minutes. (I like to put them in a small plastic container with a tight-fitting lid, so the lid keeps the mushrooms submerged.) Scoop out 2 Tbsp of the soaking water and reserve. Drain the mushrooms, discarding the remaining water, and blot the mushrooms dry with paper towels. Remove and discard the stems and cut the caps into thin strips. Set the mushrooms and reserved soaking water aside separately.

2   TO MAKE THE MARINADE: In a medium bowl, combine the cornstarch, peanut oil, garlic, rice wine, sesame oil, salt, and pepper. Whisk until the cornstarch is dissolved. Whisk in the egg white and set aside.

3   Using a very sharp, thin-bladed knife, cut the salmon fillet in half lengthwise. Cut each half crosswise into bite-size pieces about ⅓ in [12 mm] thick. Add the salmon to the marinade and stir gently to coat. Set aside.

4   In a small bowl, combine 2 Tbsp of the chicken broth and the rice wine and mix well. In a second small bowl, combine the remaining 3 Tbsp chicken broth, the reserved 2 Tbsp mushroom-soaking water, and the sesame oil and mix well. Set the two sauces aside.

Continued

5 In a wok or large, deep frying pan, heat the peanut oil over high heat and swirl to coat the bottom and sides of the pan. Add the green onions and ginger and stir-fry just until fragrant but not brown, about 10 seconds. Push the aromatics to the sides of the pan. Carefully add the salmon and spread it in a single layer. Cook undisturbed for 30 seconds. Add the chicken broth–rice wine sauce, scatter the mushrooms over the top, and cook undisturbed for 1 minute. Using a metal stir-fry spatula, gently loosen the fish without stir-frying. Add the chicken broth–sesame oil sauce and continue to cook the fish for 2 minutes. Gently turn the fish over. It should be lightly browned on the underside. Scatter the snow peas over the top, cover the pan, and cook until the snow peas are crisp-tender and bright green and the salmon is cooked through, about 1 minute longer. Do not overcook. Uncover and gently stir-fry for 10 seconds to combine the ingredients.

6 Transfer to a warmed serving dish and garnish with the lemon wedges. Serve immediately.

One 1-lb [455-g] salmon fillet, skin and pin bones removed	4 oz [115 g] smoked salmon (lox), cut into ¼-in [6-mm] dice
Fine sea salt	2 Tbsp extra-virgin olive oil
½ cup [110 g] unsalted butter, at room temperature	1 Tbsp fresh lemon juice
	1 egg yolk
1 large shallot, minced	Pinch of freshly grated nutmeg
2 Tbsp dry white wine	Freshly ground white pepper

POTTED SALMON

Serves 12 as an appetizer

In the past, meats or fish were traditionally preserved by cooking them in an abundant amount of fat and flavoring liquid. The food was often pulverized or pounded into a paste and then packed into crocks and sealed airtight with a layer of fat. The French have their rillettes and confits; the English have their potted foods. Preserving salmon this way is ideal for do-ahead entertaining, especially for the holidays. I serve this richly textured salmon with crostini or rye crackers and accompany it with cornichons, pickled onions, and pickled baby beets.

1   Cut the salmon fillet into four equal portions. Sprinkle the salmon on one side with ¼ tsp salt and let stand at room temperature for 20 minutes.

2   In a sauté pan just large enough to hold the salmon in a single layer, melt 2 Tbsp of the butter over medium-low heat. When the butter foams, add the shallot and sauté until soft but not brown, about 2 minutes. Add the salted salmon pieces in a single layer and pour the wine over the top. Cover the salmon with a piece of wax paper just slightly smaller than the diameter of the pan and then with a tight-fitting lid and cook for 2 minutes. Turn the salmon, re-cover with the wax paper and lid, and cook just until the fish turns opaque, about 2 minutes longer. Remove the pan from the heat but keep it covered and let the salmon cool in the pan.

3   In a food processor, process the remaining 6 Tbsp [85 g] butter until creamy. Use a fork to flake the cooled salmon and then add it to the butter. Add the smoked salmon and pulse the mixture just until all the ingredients are evenly mixed. The texture should be grainy; do not process until smooth. Add the olive oil, lemon juice, egg yolk, nutmeg, and a little pepper and pulse just until mixed. Taste and adjust the seasoning.

4   Pack the salmon mixture into either two 1-cup [240-ml] crocks or ramekins or one 2-cup [480-ml] ramekin. (You can also use widemouthed Mason jars.) Smooth the surface. Press a sheet of plastic wrap directly onto the salmon, forcing out any air pockets, and then press the plastic wrap against the sides of the container to seal securely. (Or, use clarified butter to seal the ramekins as described in the Cook's Note.)

5 Refrigerate the salmon for at least 2 days before serving to allow the flavors to meld. It will keep for up to 5 days if sealed with plastic wrap (or up to 8 days if sealed with clarified butter).

6 Remove the salmon from the refrigerator about 40 minutes before serving so it is not refrigerator cold.

COOK'S NOTE

To make clarified butter for sealing the potted salmon, melt ½ cup [110 g] unsalted butter in a small saucepan over medium heat. Pour the butter into a 1-cup [240-ml] glass measure and set aside until the foam rises to the top and the milky residue settles to the bottom. (If you have a microwave, skip the saucepan and melt the butter directly in a microwave-safe container.) Skim off the foam and carefully pour the clear yellow liquid into another measuring cup or small bowl. Discard the milky residue.

To seal the potted salmon with the clarified butter, pour the butter to a depth of about ⅓ in [8 mm] onto the surface of the salmon in the ramekin(s). Let the butter harden and then cover the ramekin(s) with plastic wrap and refrigerate the salmon for at least 2 days, or up to 8 days. To serve, run a paring knife around the rim of the ramekin and lift off the butter. Carefully scrape off any of the salmon mixture that adheres to the butter. (I hate to waste the butter, so I save it for frying eggs or sautéing fish. It's best to use it within a few days.)

CHAPTER 5:
IN THE
OVEN

Using the oven and broiler is a versatile and ideal way to cook salmon—whether it is slow cooking individual portions, roasting a whole fish, broiling a miso-glazed fillet, cooking sous-vide salmon without fancy equipment, or flash finishing a pan-seared fillet in a superhot oven. Some of the techniques are wonderfully simple, easy for both the confident cook and the novice. Slow-Cooked Salmon with Spring Vegetables (page 96) is just one of the recipes that nearly anyone can make with no difficulty. If easy origami sounds like fun, and you need a perfect job for young helping hands, make Salmon Baked in Parchment with Tomatoes and Corn (page 92). It's the perfect choice when the farmers' market is overrun with these two summertime vegetables.

Salmon takes on a global profile when cooked in the oven. Under the broiler, Japanese-Style Salmon Broiled with Sake and Miso Glaze (page 86) is my variation on the classic preparation made with sablefish (black cod). I like to graze; if you do too, make Broiled Sesame Salmon Bibimbap (page 87), my recipe for a Korean-style rice bowl with soy-glazed salmon.

Not everyone likes to eat salmon skin. I do, but it has to be cracker-crisp, a bit salty, and robustly flavored. Anyone who enjoys eating crisp salmon skin should immediately turn to my recipe for Crispy Salmon Skin—The Bacon of the Sea (page 102). One way I have used it is with leftover rice and salmon and fresh spinach, green onions, and ginger. I put together a tasty salmon fried rice for breakfast and topped the rice bowl with a wok-fried egg and crumbles of salmon bacon. That dish got a big thumbs-up from my husband.

Finally, although I had long wanted to learn the high-end technique of sous vide (French for "under vacuum"), I was reluctant to spend the money on an immersion circulator. After watching several videos online, I realized that I could cook salmon using sous-vide principles without the costly equipment. The delicious result is Low-Tech Sous-Vide Salmon with Sorrel Butter (page 90).

WHOLE ROASTED **SALMON** WITH LEMON, FENNEL, AND ONION

Serves 6 to 8

Nothing beats roasting a whole salmon and presenting it at the table—especially if you caught the fish. Hooking a beauty from your favorite fishmonger—which most of us will be doing—is special, too. Here are a couple of things to think about: Measure your oven so you don't buy a fish that's too large, and measure your largest rimmed baking sheet on the diagonal, because that's how you may need to position the fish. If necessary, you or the fish-monger can cut off the head of the fish. Hopefully, you won't need to cut off the tail, too, though that can be done to make this recipe work.

One 5- to 7-lb [2.3- to 3.2-kg] whole salmon, gutted, cleaned, and scaled, head and tail left on

Fine sea salt

Freshly ground black pepper

1 lemon, thinly sliced

½ yellow onion, thinly sliced

1 medium fennel bulb, trimmed, halved lengthwise, cored, and thinly sliced

1 cup [240 ml] dry white wine

½ cup [120 ml] heavy whipping cream

2 Tbsp chopped fresh dill, plus small sprigs for garnish

1 Remove the salmon from the refrigerator 30 minutes before cooking to bring it to room temperature. Measure the fish at its thickest point, usually right behind the head, to determine the cooking time.

2 Position a rack in the center of the oven and preheat the oven to 400°F [200°C]. Line the bottom and sides of an 11-by-17-in [28-by-43-cm] rimmed baking sheet with aluminum foil. Coat the foil with nonstick cooking spray.

3 Place the salmon on the prepared baking sheet, positioning it diagonally if necessary. (If the fish is still too large, use a sharp chef's knife to cut off the head. You'll find those directions on page 31.) Tilt the fish onto its back, open the cavity, and sprinkle with some salt and pepper. Return the fish back to its side and arrange half the lemon slices along the length of the cavity. Alternate and overlap the onion and fennel slices on top of the lemon, then place the remaining lemon slices on top of the onion and fennel. Pour the wine over the fish. Coat a second piece of foil with nonstick cooking spray and cover the fish completely with the foil, sprayed-side down.

4 Bake the fish for 10 minutes for every 1 in [2.5 cm] of thickness before checking for doneness. For example, if the salmon is 4 in [10 cm] thick at its thickest point, then bake for 40 minutes. Insert an instant-read thermometer into the thickest part, avoiding the spine; when it registers 120° to 125°F [49° to 52°C], the fish is done. (I prefer the fish closer to 120°F [49°C], when it is moist and just beginning to flake.)

5   Remove from the oven. Lift off and reserve the foil covering the fish. Using two large spatulas, transfer the fish to a large warmed serving platter. Cover the salmon loosely with the reserved foil to keep it warm. Pour the pan juices into a small saucepan. If you prefer to carve the fish and serve individual plates instead of presenting the salmon whole, leave the fish in the pan. Tilt the pan, using a spatula to restrain the fish, and pour off the juices into a small saucepan, then loosely re-cover the salmon with the foil.

6   Add the cream to the pan juices and bring to a simmer over medium-high heat. Simmer and reduce until the sauce has thickened and coats the back of a spoon, about 3 minutes. Stir in the chopped dill. Taste and add a little salt and pepper, if needed. Pour the sauce into a warmed small sauceboat and keep warm.

7   To serve the fish whole, peel off the top skin or leave it on. (This decision is up to the cook; you either like salmon skin or you don't.) Using a carving knife, cut along the seam running lengthwise down the middle of the backbone, then make cuts crosswise into serving-size portions. Using a knife and a serving spatula, loosen the pieces of fish. This will make it easier for your guests to serve themselves. Garnish the platter with dill sprigs before serving and pass the sauce at the table. When the top fillet has been served, lift off the backbone and ribs and then slide the onion and lemon slices to the side. Cut the bottom fillet into crosswise portions. To serve individual plates, follow the same procedure, portioning the salmon onto warmed dinner plates, spooning some sauce over top, and garnishing with a dill sprig.

¼ cup [60 ml] sake or dry white wine

¼ cup [60 ml] mirin (Japanese sweet cooking wine)

¼ cup [50 g] sugar

½ cup [120 ml] white miso paste

1 Tbsp soy sauce

1 tsp peeled and finely grated fresh ginger

6 center-cut salmon fillets, about 6 oz [170 g] each, skin and pin bones removed

SALMON
BROILED WITH SAKE AND MISO GLAZE

Serves 6

This recipe is adapted from one that appears in *Fish Forever*, Paul Johnson's award-winning cookbook. His recipe for Miso-Glazed Sablefish is one I have made on many occasions because it is simple enough for a weeknight meal and special enough for a dinner party. In fact, I often triple the marinade and keep it on hand in the refrigerator for quick-fix dinners. I typically use the marinade with the fresh-caught sablefish (black cod) purchased from Linda Brand Crab Seafood at the Portland Farmers Market. While working on this book, I decided to try the marinade with salmon, and it is an equally good pairing. Serve this dish with jasmine rice and steamed baby bok choy.

1 In a small saucepan, combine the sake, mirin, and sugar and bring to a simmer over medium heat, stirring to dissolve the sugar and evaporate the alcohol. Remove from the heat and whisk in the miso paste, soy sauce, and ginger to make a marinade. Set aside until cool.

2 Select a baking dish that is just large enough to hold the salmon in a single layer. Coat the bottom of the dish with one-third of the marinade. Arrange the salmon fillets on top and use the rest of the marinade to coat the tops and sides of the fillets. Cover with plastic wrap and refrigerate for at least 2 hours, or up to 3 hours. Remove the salmon from the refrigerator 30 minutes before cooking to bring to room temperature.

3 Position an oven rack 3 to 4 in [7.5 to 10 cm] from the heat source and preheat the broiler. Line a rimmed baking sheet with aluminum foil. Remove the salmon from the marinade, letting the excess drip off. Place the salmon, skinned-side down, on the prepared baking sheet.

4 Broil the salmon until it colors beautifully at the edges and is almost opaque throughout but still very moist, or an instant-read thermometer inserted into the center registers 115° to 120°F [45° to 49°C], 8 to 12 minutes, depending on the thickness of the fillets. The sugar in the marinade will caramelize in spots, which is desirable. If the salmon begins to char, move it farther away from the heat source to finish cooking.

5 Transfer the salmon to warmed dinner plates. Serve immediately.

BROILED SESAME SALMON BIBIMBAP

Serves 4

Bibimbap is a traditional Korean one-dish meal that marries rice, assorted vegetables, oftentimes kimchi, a raw or fried egg, seaweed strands, and, perhaps, a small amount of meat, chicken, or fish. It's the ultimate grazing bowl and a terrific way to utilize leftovers. A good-size portion of rice is spooned into a large bowl and colorful mounds of cooked ingredients are arranged on top. The popular Korean chile bean sauce known as gochujang is thinned with a little water, sweetened with a bit of sugar, and flavored with Asian sesame oil, vinegar, and some-times garlic and served as a sauce with the dish. Look for gochujang in Korean markets, in Asian markets selling Korean foods, or online. Chinese chile bean sauce is a fine substitute.

SALMON

One 12-oz [340-g] salmon fillet, skin on and scaled, pin bones removed

1 Tbsp soy sauce

2 Tbsp unseasoned rice vinegar

¼ cup [60 ml] mirin (Japanese sweet cooking wine)

1 tsp peeled and finely grated fresh ginger

1 tsp sesame seeds, toasted

⅛ tsp freshly ground black pepper

VEGETABLES

Fine sea salt

4 oz [115 g] bean sprouts

8 oz [230 g] baby spinach

2 tsp soy sauce

1 tsp Asian sesame oil

2 tsp sesame seeds, toasted

4 tsp grapeseed or other neutral oil

8 oz [230 g] shiitake mushrooms, stems removed, caps cut into thin strips

4 tsp mirin (Japanese sweet cooking wine)

2 carrots, peeled and cut into matchsticks

BIBIMBAP SAUCE

¼ cup [60 ml] gochujang (Korean chile bean sauce) or Chinese chile bean sauce

2 Tbsp water

2 Tbsp sugar

4 tsp Asian sesame oil

2 tsp unseasoned rice vinegar

4 cups hot steamed rice

4 wok-fried eggs (optional)

1 **TO PREPARE THE SALMON:** Place the fillet in a nonreactive pan just large enough to hold it. In a small bowl, combine the soy sauce, vinegar, mirin, ginger, sesame seeds, and pepper and mix well. Pour the marinade over the salmon, then turn the salmon to coat all sides. (Alternatively, place the salmon in a freezer-strength lock-top plastic bag, pour in the marinade, press to remove any air from the bag, and seal tightly. Turn the bag to coat the salmon on all sides with the marinade.) Marinate the salmon at room temperature for at least 30 min-utes but no more than 1 hour.

2 **MEANWHILE, PREPARE THE VEGETABLES:** Fill a large saucepan two-thirds full of water and bring to a boil over high heat. Add 1 tsp salt and then add the bean sprouts and cook for 1 minute. Using a slotted spoon, transfer the sprouts to a colander to drain. Blot the sprouts with paper towels and transfer to a small bowl.

Continued

3 Add the spinach to the same boiling water and cook just until bright green and wilted, about 1 minute. Drain the spinach in the colander and place under cold running water to stop the cooking. Shake off the excess water. When the spinach is cool, squeeze out the excess liquid and transfer the spinach to a medium bowl.

4 Toss the sprouts with ½ tsp of the soy sauce and ¼ tsp of the sesame oil. Set aside. Toss the spinach with 1 tsp of the soy sauce, ¼ tsp of the sesame oil, and the sesame seeds. Set aside.

5 In a wok or a large, deep frying pan, heat 2 tsp of the grapeseed oil over high heat and swirl to coat the bottom and sides of the pan. Add the mushrooms and stir-fry for 1 minute. Add 2 tsp of the mirin, ¼ tsp of the sesame oil, and the remaining ½ tsp soy sauce. Stir-fry until the mushrooms are browned and softened, about 2 minutes longer. Transfer to a plate. Add the remaining 2 tsp grapeseed oil to the pan over high heat and swirl to coat the bottom and sides of the pan. Add the carrots and stir-fry for 2 minutes. Add a pinch of salt and the remaining 2 tsp mirin and ¼ tsp sesame oil. Stir-fry until crisp-tender, about 1 minute longer. Transfer to a plate and set aside.

6 TO MAKE THE SAUCE: In a small bowl, combine the gochujang, water, sugar, sesame oil, and vinegar and mix well. Set aside until ready to serve.

7 Position an oven rack 3 to 4 in [7.5 to 10 cm] from the heat source and preheat the broiler. Line a rimmed baking sheet with aluminum foil. Remove the salmon from the marinade, wiping off any excess. Place the salmon, skin-side down, on the prepared baking sheet.

8 Broil the salmon until it begins to color, about 3 minutes. Turn the salmon skin-side up and cook until almost opaque throughout but still very moist, or an instant-read thermometer inserted into the center registers 115° to 120°F [45° to 49°C], 3 to 4 minutes longer. (Don't worry if the skin starts to char; it will be removed before serving.)

9 Remove the salmon from the broiler. Lift off the skin and discard it or chop some of the crispy pieces and reserve for garnishing the bowls. Cut the salmon into four equal portions.

10 Divide the rice evenly among warmed bowls. Top each serving of rice with a portion of salmon, arranging it to one side of the bowl. Arrange the vegetables—bean sprouts, spinach, mushrooms, carrots—in individual mounds around the sides of the bowl. Slip in a wok-fried egg, if desired. Spoon some of the sauce onto the center of each bowl and garnish with some crisp salmon skin, if you like. Serve immediately.

LOW-TECH SOUS-VIDE SALMON WITH SORREL BUTTER

Serves 4 to 6

My first attempt at cooking salmon sous vide was in the most low-tech way possible. I cobbled together my method by watching several videos on the Internet. It worked perfectly, and now I am hooked. A favorite of many restaurant chefs, this technique of vacuum-sealing food and cooking it at a precise low temperature for a long period of time is now accessible to the home cook. You can buy the high-tech equipment (I did as soon as the price dropped to reasonable levels), but you don't really need it for salmon because the fish cooks in less than a half hour. In that short amount of time, placing a roasting pan filled with water heated to 118°F [48°C] in an oven set at its lowest heat setting will maintain the temperature of the water for the relatively brief time the salmon needs to cook. This low-tech method is easy and surefire, and I am excited to share it with you.

Serve the salmon on a bed of sautéed greens or with a purée of potatoes or celery root. It would also be delicious with the potato and kale mash on page 94.

SORREL BUTTER

1 cup [220 g] unsalted butter, at room temperature, thinly sliced

1½ cups [60 g] finely chopped fresh sorrel leaves (see Cook's Note)

1 tsp fine sea salt

1 tsp finely ground black pepper

Grated zest of 1 lemon

4 to 6 center-cut salmon fillets, about 6 oz [170 g] each, skin and pin bones removed, brined (see page 40; optional)

4 to 6 tsp extra-virgin olive oil

Fine sea salt

Freshly ground black pepper

You will also need

Four to six 1-qt [1-L] freezer-strength lock-top plastic bags

1 **TO MAKE THE SORREL BUTTER:** In a food processor, scatter half the butter around the work bowl, put the sorrel, salt, pepper, and lemon zest on top, and then add the rest of the butter. Process until all the ingredients are evenly distributed, stopping the machine once or twice to scrape down the sides of the bowl.

2 Lay a sheet of plastic wrap or parchment paper on a clean work surface. Using a rubber spatula, transfer the butter from the work bowl to the plastic wrap. Then, still using the spatula, form the butter into a rough log about 1½ in [4 cm] in diameter. Wrap the plastic wrap around the butter, roll to form a smooth, compact log, and twist the ends closed. Refrigerate for up to 5 days or freeze for up to 3 months.

3 Remove the salmon from the refrigerator 30 minutes before cooking to bring it to room temperature.

4 Position a rack in the center of the oven and set the oven to the lowest heat setting possible, typically 150° to 175°F [65° to 80°C]. Fill a roasting pan or large Dutch oven two-thirds full of water, place on the stove top over medium heat, and heat until the water registers about 125°F [52°C] on an instant-read thermometer. Remove from the heat.

5 While the water is heating, rub each fillet all over with 1 tsp of the olive oil, then lightly season each fillet on both sides with salt and pepper. Place each fillet, skinned-side down, in its own lock-top plastic bag. Cut four to six slices of the sorrel butter, each ¼ in [6 mm] thick. (Reserve the remaining sorrel butter for another use; it is delicious on chicken and steamed vegetables.) Place a disk of butter on top of each fillet.

6 One at a time, lay each bag flat on a clean work surface and use both hands to press down firmly on the bag all around the fillet, forcing out all of the air. Seal the bag securely.

7 Check the water temperature in the pan. By now it should have dropped to close to the desired temperature of 118°F [48°C]. If not, add a bit of cool water. Submerge each bag in the water. (If a bag floats, lift it out of the water, open it, press out the air again, and reseal it.) Carefully transfer the pan to the oven. Set a timer and cook the salmon for 25 minutes. To check for doneness, lift out one of the bags, carefully open it, and insert an instant-read thermometer into the center of the fillet. The salmon is done when it registers between 115° and 120°F [45° and 49°C].

8 Use a spatula to lift each fillet out of its bag and place it in the center of a warmed shallow pasta bowl. Spoon the sauce from the bag over the top. Serve immediately.

COOK'S NOTE

Look for sorrel, a lemony-tasting hardy perennial herb, at your local farmers' market in the spring, early summer, and fall. Or, better yet, buy a plant or seeds and grow your own. I do not have a gardener's green thumb but, despite my lack of attention, the sorrel I planted grew abundantly in a container of herbs in a semi-shady spot on my back porch.

SALMON
BAKED IN PARCHMENT WITH TOMATOES AND CORN

Serves 4

Baking in parchment, *en papillote* in French, is food tucked inside a sealed packet of parchment and baked until the paper puffs and the edges brown. The glory of this technique is that all the healthful goodness and freshness of the food bakes inside. It is a dramatic presentation, easy to master. Folding the parchment to seal the packets tightly is like easy origami. Practice once with a sheet of parchment and you'll have it mastered. If working with parchment feels intimidating or you don't have any on hand, you can use aluminum foil. The folds are a cinch to do with foil, but the presentation isn't as elegant. If you choose foil and don't like how it looks, you can unwrap the packets in the kitchen and arrange the salmon and vegetables directly on warmed dinner plates.

4 center-cut salmon fillets, about 5 oz [140 g] each, skin and pin bones removed

Extra-virgin olive oil for rubbing and drizzling

Fine sea salt

Freshly ground black pepper

1½ cups [190 g] fresh corn kernels

1½ cups [230 g] orange or red cherry tomatoes, halved

2 green onions, including green tops, thinly sliced crosswise

1 Tbsp drained brined capers, rinsed and patted dry

2 tsp fresh thyme leaves, plus 4 sprigs

1 large lemon; ½ for squeezing, ½ sliced into paper-thin rounds

1 Remove the salmon from the refrigerator 30 minutes before cooking to bring it to room temperature.

2 Position a rack in the center of the oven and preheat the oven to 450°F [230°C]. Have ready a large rimmed baking sheet and four 12-by-16-in [30.5-by-40.5-cm] sheets of parchment paper or aluminum foil. Fold each sheet in half to form a 12-by-8-in [30.5-by-20-cm] rectangle. Crease the fold and then spread each sheet back open. Set aside.

3 Rub each salmon fillet all over with a little olive oil. Season each fillet on both sides with salt and pepper.

4 In a medium bowl, combine the corn, tomatoes, green onions, capers, and thyme leaves. Drizzle a little olive oil over the top and season with a pinch of salt and a little pepper. (The capers will be salty, so go lightly on the salt.) Stir to combine.

5 Arrange the creased parchment on a work surface, positioning each sheet so a long side is facing you. For each packet, place one-fourth of the corn mixture in a mound just below the crease. Place a salmon fillet on top of each mound of vegetables. Using the lemon half, squeeze a little lemon juice over each fillet. Top each fillet with two or three lemon slices, overlapping them, and a thyme sprig.

6 Fold the top half of the parchment over the salmon and vegetables to enclose them. To seal each packet, begin at one corner near the creased edge. Fold the edge over to form a small triangle and then move down and make overlapping folds, one on top of the other, all around the edge of the packet to seal it, ending up at the other creased edge. Here, at the last folded edge, twist and tuck the corner under the parchment to secure it closed. Place the packets on the baking sheet.

7 Bake until the packets puff up, about 8 minutes for thinner fillets and 10 minutes for thicker ones. (The parchment packets will turn brown around the edges.) The salmon will be cooked through and medium-rare at the center. Bake for 2 minutes longer if you prefer your salmon more well-done.

8 Place each packet on a warmed dinner plate. Using the tip of a sharp knife, cut an *X* in the top of each packet, preferably at the table for a more dramatic presentation. Serve immediately.

PAN-ROASTED SALMON WITH POTATOES AND KALE

Serves 6

Salmon fishing is part of the Irish identity and so is this celebrated potato and kale dish known as colcannon. Let them be paired in perfect harmony for this terrific one-dish meal. Pan roasting is a restaurant-style, two-step technique worth mastering. The skin side of the salmon fillet is browned in a cast-iron frying pan on top of the stove and then quickly moved to a hot oven to finish cooking. What this high-heat roasting technique delivers is beautifully seared and deliciously crisp salmon skin with perfectly moist, flaky flesh.

6 center-cut salmon fillets, about 6 oz [170 g] each, skin on and scaled, pin bones removed, skin-dried (see page 40)

2 lb [910 g] russet or other floury potatoes

Fine sea salt

7 Tbsp [100 g] unsalted butter

2 to 3 cups [50 to 75 g] lightly packed chopped kale leaves

1¼ cups [300 ml] milk

4 green onions, green tops only, minced

Freshly ground black pepper

⅓ cup [40 g] Wondra (see Cook's Note, page 76) or white rice flour

3 Tbsp grapeseed or other neutral oil

1 lemon, halved and seeded

2 Tbsp chopped fresh dill

1 Remove the salmon from the refrigerator 30 minutes before cooking to bring it to room temperature.

2 Position a rack in the center of the oven and preheat the oven to 450°F [230°C].

3 Put the potatoes in a large pot and add water to cover by at least 1 in [2.5 cm]. Add 2 tsp salt, place over high heat, and bring to a boil. Lower the heat to a simmer, cover partially, and cook the potatoes until very tender when pierced with a fork, about 30 minutes.

4 Meanwhile, in a large sauté pan, warm 4 Tbsp [55 g] of the butter over medium-high heat. Add the kale and cook, stirring frequently, until wilted, about 5 minutes. Set aside.

5 In a medium saucepan, heat the milk just until hot but not boiling. Add 2 Tbsp of the butter and the green onions and simmer for 2 minutes. Add the kale, using a heat-resistant rubber spatula to scrape any excess butter from the sauté pan into the milk mixture. Stir well to combine, remove from the heat, cover, and keep warm.

6 When the potatoes are ready, drain them in a colander and let stand until just cool enough to handle, about 10 minutes. Use a paring knife to slip off the skins and then return the potatoes to the pan. Mash with a potato masher. Stir the milk mixture into the potatoes and mash to distribute the kale evenly. Season with salt and pepper. Keep warm while you prepare and cook the salmon.

7 Blot the salmon dry with paper towels. Season both sides of each salmon fillet with salt and pepper. Spread the flour in a pie plate or a wide, shallow bowl. Dip the skin side of each fillet in the flour, shaking off the excess. As the fillets are coated, set them aside, coated-side up, on a plate.

8 Place a large ovenproof frying pan, preferably cast iron, over medium-high heat. When the pan is hot, add the grapeseed oil and swirl to coat the bottom of the pan. When the oil is hot but not smoking, add the salmon fillets, skin-side down, then press down on each fillet with the back of a metal spatula to maximize the contact with the surface of the pan. (This helps crisp the skin.) Cook on one side, without disturbing, until the skin is golden and crisp, about 3 minutes. Turn the fillets skin-side up and transfer the frying pan to the oven. Roast the salmon until almost opaque throughout but still very moist, or an instant-read thermometer inserted into the center registers 115° to 120°F [45° to 49°C], 3 to 4 minutes longer.

9 Melt the remaining 1 Tbsp butter. Divide the potato mixture evenly among warmed dinner plates, mounding it in the center. Place a salmon fillet, skin-side up, on top of each mound. Drizzle a little butter over each portion of salmon and potatoes. Squeeze some lemon juice on top and garnish with the dill. Serve immediately.

SLOW-COOKED SALMON WITH SPRING VEGETABLES

Serves 4

Along with April's springtime showers comes the anticipation of freshly dug baby carrots, tender shoots of asparagus, young spring leeks, and sweet English peas at the farmers' market. It's time to celebrate the season with a dish that goes together easily for a weeknight supper and is festive enough for a dinner with friends. Do all your prep work in advance, and you'll be ready to serve this main course in less than a half hour.

4 center-cut salmon fillets, about 6 oz [170 g] each, skin and pin bones removed

Extra-virgin olive oil for rubbing

Fine sea salt

Freshly ground black pepper

Pinch of cayenne pepper

2 cups [480 ml] dry white wine

½ cup [120 ml] water

20 petite carrots with tops, trimmed, leaving ½-in [12-mm] green stem attached

1 leek, white and pale green parts, sliced ¼ in [6 mm] thick

16 slender asparagus spears, tough bottoms discarded, cut into 2-in [5-cm] lengths

½ cup [110 g] unsalted butter, at room temperature, cut into chunks

½ cup [70 g] fresh or frozen green peas, rinsed under hot water if frozen

1 Tbsp chopped fresh mint, plus more for garnish

1. Remove the salmon from the refrigerator 30 minutes before cooking to bring it to room temperature. Pat dry with paper towels.

2. Position a rack in the center of the oven and preheat the oven to 250°F [120°C]. Line a small rimmed baking sheet or baking pan with parchment paper.

3. Arrange the salmon fillets on the prepared baking sheet. Rub each fillet all over with olive oil and season with salt and black pepper and the cayenne.

4. Bake the salmon until it is almost opaque throughout but still very moist, or an instant-read thermometer inserted into the center registers 115° to 120°F [45° to 49°C], 15 to 20 minutes. (When the salmon is cooked gently at such a low temperature, it looks underdone because the color is so beautifully pink and vivid, but it is fully cooked.)

5. While the salmon is baking, set a 10-in [25-cm] frying pan over medium-high heat, add the wine and water, and bring to a boil. Add the carrots, leek, and ½ tsp salt. Turn the heat to medium and simmer until the carrots are crisp-tender, 12 to 15 minutes.

6. Meanwhile, fill a small saucepan two-thirds full with lightly salted water and bring to a boil over high heat. Add the asparagus, adjust the heat to a simmer, and cook until the asparagus is crisp-tender and bright green, 3 to 4 minutes. Drain in a colander, rinse under cold running water, and blot dry.

Continued

7 When the carrots are tender, remove the pan from the heat. Using a heat-resistant rubber spatula, stir the butter, a chunk at a time, into the wine mixture until emulsified. Season with salt and black pepper. Return the pan to the heat and add the asparagus and peas. Warm just until the asparagus and peas are heated through. Stir in the mint.

8 Divide the vegetables and sauce evenly among warmed shallow pasta bowls. Place a salmon fillet on top and garnish with a little mint. Serve immediately.

PANKO-CRUSTED SALMON CAKES WITH JICAMA ORANGE SLAW

Makes 12 salmon cakes; serves 12 as an appetizer or 6 as a main course

Just like perfect crab cakes that fall apart with the touch of a fork, these salmon cakes have no heavy binders and aren't bogged down with bread crumbs or other fillers. The fresh taste of the salmon, accented with ginger, onion, and herbs, makes these cakes light and delectable, and coating them in panko (Japanese bread crumbs) gives them a delectable crisp crust. As a nice contrast and welcome addition to the plate, I've added a citrus-infused jicama slaw with orange segments, red onion, and lots of cilantro. Although the ingredients list looks long, the salmon cakes and slaw are quick to make, and there are lots of do-ahead options. Plus, they are intensely good!

One 12-oz [340-g] salmon fillet, skin and pin bones removed

2 tsp extra-virgin olive oil

Fine sea salt

Freshly ground black pepper

4 Tbsp [55 g] unsalted butter

1 Tbsp peeled and minced fresh ginger

½ cup [70 g] finely diced white onion

½ cup [70 g] finely diced celery

½ cup [70 g] finely diced red bell pepper

½ cup [120 ml] mayonnaise

1 Tbsp fresh lemon juice

¼ tsp cayenne pepper

1 tsp minced fresh thyme

2 tsp snipped fresh chives

2 Tbsp minced fresh flat-leaf parsley

JICAMA ORANGE SLAW

One 12-oz [340-g] jicama, peeled and cut into matchsticks 2 in [5 cm] long and ¼ in [6 mm] thick

½ small red onion, halved lengthwise and cut into thin wedges

3 satsuma oranges, peeled, white pith removed, and sectioned

⅓ cup [10 g] chopped fresh cilantro

3 Tbsp extra-virgin olive oil

Juice of 1 lime

1 tsp Dijon mustard

¾ tsp ground cumin

¾ tsp fine sea salt

½ tsp sugar

Freshly ground black pepper

1½ cups [90 g] panko (Japanese bread crumbs)

2 Tbsp grapeseed or other neutral oil

1 Position a rack in the center of the oven and preheat the oven to 250°F [120°C].

2 Place the salmon in a shallow baking dish just large enough to hold it. Rub it all over with the olive oil and season lightly with salt and black pepper.

3 Bake the salmon until the fat between the layers turns opaque, almost white, and the fish flakes slightly when pierced with a knife, about 20 minutes. Alternatively, insert an instant-read thermometer into the thickest part of the salmon; when it registers about 125°F [52°C], the fish is done. Set aside to cool.

Continued

4   Meanwhile, in a nonstick frying pan or sauté pan, melt 2 Tbsp of the butter over medium heat and swirl to coat the bottom of the pan. Add the ginger, white onion, celery, and bell pepper and sauté, stirring frequently, until the vegetables are soft but not brown, about 4 minutes. Add ½ tsp salt and a few grinds of black pepper. Set aside to cool.

5   In a medium bowl, combine the mayonnaise, lemon juice, cayenne, thyme, chives, and parsley and mix well. Using a fork, flake the salmon into small pieces and add it to the mayonnaise mixture. Add the cooled vegetables and, using a rubber spatula, gently mix the ingredients, being careful not to mash the salmon.

6   Form the salmon mixture into 12 cakes, each about 1¾ in [4.5 cm] in diameter and ½ in [12 mm] thick. Place the salmon cakes on a rimmed baking sheet, cover, and refrigerate for at least 40 minutes, or up to 8 hours.

7   TO MAKE THE SLAW: In a large bowl, combine the jicama, red onion, oranges, and cilantro and toss to mix well. In a small bowl, combine the olive oil, lime juice, mustard, cumin, salt, sugar, and a few grinds of black pepper and stir vigorously to form a dressing. Taste and adjust the seasoning. Pour the dressing over the slaw and toss to mix well. Cover and refrigerate for up to 1 day. Remove from the refrigerator 30 minutes before serving. Toss again just before serving.

8   Spread the panko on a dinner plate. One at a time, roll the salmon cakes in the panko, coating evenly on all sides, then set aside on a plate. In a large sauté pan, preferably cast iron, heat the remaining 2 Tbsp butter and the grapeseed oil over medium-high heat and swirl to coat the bottom of the pan. Working in batches to avoid crowding, brown the salmon cakes on one side, about 3 minutes. Flip them and brown the second side, about 3 minutes longer. Transfer to a plate and keep warm. Repeat with the remaining cakes.

9   Serve the salmon cakes warm, accompanied with the slaw.

3 Tbsp soy sauce

2 Tbsp water

2 Tbsp firmly packed golden brown sugar

1 Tbsp fresh lemon juice

Scaled skin from 1 or 2 sides of salmon fillet

CRISPY SALMON SKIN— THE BACON OF THE SEA

Makes 1 or 2 crispy salmon skins from a whole fish or fillet; yield varies based on amount of salmon skin used

There are two types of salmon eaters: the ones who like to eat crisp salmon skin and the ones who think eating the skin in any form is disgusting. If you don't like salmon skin, skip this recipe. If you love crackly crisp salmon skin, make this recipe. It's divine and really is the bacon of the sea. I crumble it and scatter it over main-course salmon salads or rice bowls. Best of all, I strew it over poached eggs accompanied with sautéed greens and hot-pepper sauce. But you can use it over anything you would sprinkle crumbled bacon over.

1 In a small saucepan over medium heat, combine the soy sauce, water, and brown sugar and bring to a boil, stirring until the sugar is dissolved. Remove from the heat and add the lemon juice. Set the marinade aside to cool.

2 Meanwhile, stretch the salmon skin, flesh-side up, on a cutting board. Using a paring knife, carefully scrape away any bits of salmon fat or flesh. (This is important because the skin won't crisp if it isn't scraped clean.) Transfer the skin to a 1-qt [1-L] freezer-strength lock-top plastic bag. Pour the marinade over the skin, force all the air out of the bag, and seal the bag. Refrigerate for at least 3 hours, or, preferably, overnight. Remove the bag from the refrigerator 1 hour before baking.

3 Position a rack in the lower third of the oven and preheat the oven to 275°F [135°C]. Line a baking sheet with aluminum foil and generously coat the foil with nonstick cooking spray.

4 Remove the salmon skin from the marinade, draining off the excess. Discard the marinade. Stretch the salmon skin on the prepared baking sheet so it is perfectly flat, pressing down on the edges if they have curled up.

5 Bake the skin for 30 minutes and then check the progress. At this point, the skin should still be flabby. Continue to bake the skin, checking it every 10 minutes, until it is crisp and dry. The drying time will vary between 40 and 60 minutes, depending on humidity and the accuracy of the oven temperature. You want the sugar to caramelize but not burn, so keep a close eye on the skin toward the end of cooking.

6 When the skin is ready, set the pan aside until the skin cools, then carefully remove it from the foil. Break it into shards and serve. It is best used the day it is made, though it can be wrapped in foil and set aside at room temperature for up to 1 day. To re-crisp the skin, sandwich it between two sheets of foil and set it under the broiler to heat through and crisp.

CHAPTER 6:
ON THE GRILL

Mastering salmon on the grill can be a challenge. You can learn a handful of techniques to ensure success, however, and that's what this chapter is all about. While developing the recipes for this cookbook, I sometimes thought I was going to grow gills because I was cooking and eating so much salmon. But all that trial and error resulted in my perfecting techniques that are good not only for salmon but for all seafood on the grill. Here are some simple strategies for perfectly grilled salmon.

Salmon has a high oil content, which helps keep it moist on the grill. That said, the flesh is tender and it can stick to the grill grate and tear when you try to turn over a fillet. Instead of placing salmon directly on the grate, I use planks, cedar sheets, skewers, banana leaves, a fish-shaped grill basket, a plancha, and even a bed of fresh herbs to help keep the fish from sticking. Cedar or alder planks infuse fish with a subtle and appealing wood-smoked flavor. The same is true for cedar sheets; plus, opening a slightly charred, paper-thin wood sheet to reveal a fish fillet is spectacular. Skewers allow you to maneuver small chunks of fish or whole shellfish easily, and grilling fish on a bed of sturdy herbs, such as rosemary or thyme, imparts a lovely aroma and provides a barrier between the flesh and the grate.

WHOLE SALMON ON THE GRILL WITH LEMON AND BAY LAUREL

Serves 6 to 8

Grilling a whole salmon in a grill basket is the surefire way to achieve a beautifully crisp-skinned, moist fish that doesn't stick to the grill grate. My favorite style of grill basket is a large fish-shaped cage. Although the baskets come in different sizes, I prefer one large enough to hold a good-size sockeye salmon. They are hinged on one end and have wire handles on the other end that clasp together when the basket is closed. They also have metal feet on both sides so the basket sits up off the grill grate. If you oil the skin of the fish and use nonstick spray on the grill basket, you'll be able to remove the fish without the skin tearing. A grill basket works equally well for cooking a whole side of salmon.

One 5- to 7-lb [2.3- to 3.2-kg] whole salmon, preferably sockeye, gutted, cleaned, and scaled, head removed and tail left on, skin-dried (see page 40)

Fine sea salt

Freshly ground black pepper

16 fresh bay leaves, or dried leaves soaked in warm water for 20 minutes

1 small yellow onion, cut into thin rounds

1 lemon, sliced paper-thin

Extra-virgin olive oil for brushing

You will also need

Large fish-shaped grill basket

1 Remove the salmon from the refrigerator 30 minutes before grilling to bring it to room temperature. Pat dry with paper towels.

2 Prepare a medium fire in a charcoal grill or preheat a gas grill to medium. Coat the grill basket with nonstick cooking spray. Check to see if the salmon will fit comfortably, albeit snuggly, in the grill basket. If the salmon is too long, trim off the tail.

3 Sprinkle the fish cavity generously with salt and pepper. Lay half of the bay leaves in a line along the length of the cavity. Overlap the onion rounds on top of the bay leaves. Overlap the lemon slices on top of the onion, and then arrange the remaining bay leaves in a line on top of the lemon. Brush or rub the skin of the salmon all over with olive oil and sprinkle lightly with salt and pepper. Securely close the basket.

4 The internal temperature of the grill should be about 425°F [220°C]. If needed, bank the coals to one side of the charcoal grill or turn off one of the burners of the gas grill to attain that temperature when the grill is covered. Place the grill basket directly over the fire and cover the grill. Grill the salmon on one side until the skin is crisp and brown, about 10 minutes. Turn the basket over and grill the fish on the other side until it is almost opaque throughout but still very moist, or an instant-read thermometer inserted in the center away from the spine registers about 120°F [49°C], about 8 minutes longer.

Continued

5 Transfer the basket to a heat-resistant surface. Unlatch the grill basket slowly to avoid tearing the skin. Use a table knife to release any skin sticking to the wires. Carefully lift and transfer the salmon to a warmed serving platter.

6 To serve the fish whole, peel off the top skin or leave it on. (This decision is up to the cook; you either like salmon skin or you don't.) Using a carving knife, cut along the seam running lengthwise down the middle of the backbone, then make cuts crosswise into serving-size portions. Using a knife and a serving spatula, loosen the pieces of fish. This will make it easier for your guests to serve themselves. When the top fillet has been served, lift off the backbone and ribs and then slide the bay leaves and onion and lemon slices to the side. Cut the bottom fillet into crosswise portions. To serve individual plates, follow the same procedure, portioning the salmon onto warmed dinner plates.

HERE ARE A FEW MORE GRILLING TIPS THAT WILL GUARANTEE SUCCESS:

- Start with a clean, hot, well-oiled grill grate. Small bits of charred food left on the grate will stick to a raw fish fillet and tear the flesh when you try to move it. Preheat the grate; brush it so it is clean, clean, clean; and then oil the grate until it is well coated and slick.

- Even if the fish has been seasoned with an oil-based marinade, paste, or rub, brush it or rub it on all sides with oil before putting it on the grill. This step is critical to successful fish grilling. Don't be afraid to give the fillets a good coating. It won't make the fish oily, and it will prevent it from sticking.

- Use a wide spatula or a fish spatula to turn fillets, and use tongs to turn skewers. Salmon fillets need to be supported when they are turned, so having the correct tool is important. Also, turn fillets only once. The less you move them, the less likely they are to fall apart.

- The timings in the recipes are only guidelines, as every grill—and every fire—is slightly different. Lift the edge of a fillet to see if the flesh on the underside is nicely seared with beautiful grill marks and, if it is, turn the fillet. Check for doneness with an instant-read thermometer.

SALMON
A LA PLANCHA WITH CITRUS-DILL-VODKA MARINADE

Serves 6

In Spain, cooking *a la plancha*—grilled on a metal plate—is a time-honored technique for preparing fish. Although free-form metal sheets were regularly used in the past, and sometimes still are, cast-iron griddles with a smooth surface are a better choice. I have a well-seasoned, large rectangular griddle that fits over two burners of my gas stove top and also works well on my outdoor grill. It is great not only for fish and seafood but also for vegetables that tend to fall through the bars of the grill grate and for flatbreads. It measures almost 20 in [50 cm] long and is 10 in [25 cm] wide and is the perfect size for a whole side of salmon. When the surface is smoking hot, the skin on the salmon sizzles the moment it touches the pan.

1 whole side of salmon, about 3 lb [1.4 kg], skin on and scaled, pin bones removed

¼ cup [60 ml] extra-virgin olive oil, plus more for rubbing

2 Tbsp vodka

Grated zest of 1 lemon, plus 2 Tbsp fresh lemon juice

2 Tbsp chopped fresh dill

½ tsp fine sea salt

½ tsp freshly ground black pepper

You will also need

Plancha (large, rectangular griddle)

1 Remove the salmon from the refrigerator 30 minutes before grilling to bring it to room temperature. Pat dry with paper towels.

2 Prepare a medium-hot fire in a charcoal grill or preheat a gas grill to medium-high.

3 In a small bowl, combine the olive oil, vodka, lemon zest, lemon juice, dill, salt, and pepper and mix well to form a marinade.

4 Place the salmon, flesh-side down, on a large, rimmed baking sheet. Rub the skin generously with olive oil. Turn the salmon over, flesh-side up, and pour the marinade evenly over the top. Set aside while the grill heats.

5 When ready to grill, place the plancha on the grill grate directly over the fire and cover the grill. After 10 minutes, the plancha should be smoking hot. (If your plancha is well seasoned, there is no need to oil the surface. If it is new, brush it with oil to be sure the skin of the fish won't stick.) Uncover the grill, transfer the salmon, skin-side down, to the plancha, and re-cover the grill. Grill the salmon, without turning it, until it is almost opaque throughout but still very moist, or an instant-read thermometer inserted into the center registers 115° to 120°F [45° to 49°C], 15 to 20 minutes, depending on the thickness of the fillet.

6 Using two long spatulas, transfer the salmon to a warmed platter. Serve the whole side of salmon on the platter family-style, or cut the salmon into individual portions and transfer to warmed dinner plates. (I let the plancha cool down in place, or use tongs, heatproof gloves, or the spatulas to move the plancha to a heatproof surface to cool.)

ALDER-PLANKED **SALMON** WITH LEMON, ROSEMARY, AND THYME

Serves 6 to 8

For hundreds of years, Native Americans living in the Pacific Northwest have cooked salmon on wood planks. They build a huge fire pit, attach sides of salmon to planks, and then drive the bottom of each plank into the ground so the salmon slowly grill-roasts vertically next to the fire. The technique I describe here is much simpler. Grilling salmon on a wood plank imparts a sweet, smoky, slightly charred flavor to the fish. The possibilities for flavor depend on the type of wood you use—alder, cedar, or oak—and the sauce, marinade, or rub you choose. Use this recipe as a guide. It explains the basic technique of grilling fish on a plank and delivers a fresh and flavorful combination of herbs and sweet smokiness. The variations are countless.

1 whole side of salmon, about 3 lb [1.4 kg], skin on and scaled, pin bones removed

Extra-virgin olive oil for rubbing

Fine sea salt

Freshly ground black pepper

Leaves from 4 sprigs fresh thyme

Leaves from 4 sprigs fresh rosemary, coarsely chopped

½ lemon

You will also need

Untreated alder plank, about 15 by 7 by ⅜ in [38 by 17 by 1 cm] (see Cook's Note)

1 Rinse the plank and place it in a pan, sink, or large leakproof plastic bag filled with water. Soak the plank for about 40 minutes. (The plank can be submerged in water and left to soak all day, so if possible, plan ahead and soak the plank before you leave for work.)

2 Remove the salmon from the refrigerator 30 minutes before grilling to bring it to room temperature. Pat dry with paper towels.

3 Prepare a medium fire in a charcoal grill or preheat a gas grill to medium.

4 Place the salmon on a large rimmed baking sheet. Rub all over with olive oil and sprinkle lightly on both sides with salt and pepper. Position the salmon skin-side down and scatter the thyme and rosemary leaves over the flesh side, pressing them gently so they adhere. Set aside while the grill heats.

5 When ready to grill, place the soaked plank on the grill grate directly over the fire and cover the grill. After a few minutes, the plank will begin to smoke and crackle. Turn the plank over, re-cover the grill, and "toast" the other side for about 2 minutes. Uncover the grill, transfer the salmon, flesh-side up, to the plank, and re-cover the grill. Grill the salmon until it is almost opaque throughout but still very moist, or an instant-read thermometer inserted into the center registers 115° to 120°F [45° to 49°C], 15 to 25 minutes, depending on the thickness of the fillet. (Keep a spray bottle filled with water nearby in case the plank gets too hot and begins to flame. Spritz the plank to extinguish the flame and continue grilling the salmon, adjusting the heat level if necessary.)

6 Using two long spatulas, transfer the salmon to a warmed platter. (Use tongs, heatproof gloves, or the spatulas to move the plank to a heatproof surface to cool.) Squeeze the juice from the lemon half over the salmon, then cut the salmon into individual portions. Alternatively, for a rustic presentation, leave the salmon on the plank and place the plank on a large heatproof platter. Serve immediately.

COOK'S NOTES

Buy precut planks specifically for grilling or baking salmon at gourmet cookware stores, high-end grocery stores, or online. Or, for a slightly less expensive approach, purchase untreated alder, cedar, or oak shingles from lumberyards or hardware stores, trim them to size, and give them a quick once-over with sandpaper.

A plank can be reused if it isn't too charred or cracked. Once the plank has cooled, brush it clean with a grill brush, set it upright to dry, and then store it in a brown paper bag. Soak it again before using.

4 center-cut salmon fillets, about 6 oz [170 g] each, skin on and scaled, pin bones removed

Extra-virgin olive oil for brushing

Fine sea salt

Freshly ground black pepper

8 sprigs fresh thyme

8 sprigs fresh rosemary

1 lemon, cut into 8 thin slices

1 Remove the salmon from the refrigerator 30 minutes before grilling to bring it to room temperature. Pat dry with paper towels.

2 Prepare a medium fire in a charcoal grill or preheat a gas grill to medium.

3 Generously brush the salmon fillets on both sides with olive oil and sprinkle lightly on both sides with salt and pepper. Crisscross two thyme sprigs and two rosemary sprigs on the flesh side of each fillet, pressing them lightly so they adhere to the flesh.

4 When ready to grill, generously oil the grill grate. Use tongs to arrange the salmon fillets, herb-side down, directly over the fire and cover the grill. Grill the salmon until grill marks are etched across the fillets on the underside, about 3 minutes. Turn the fillets skin-side down, re-cover the grill, and cook until the salmon is almost opaque throughout but still very moist, or an instant-read thermometer inserted into the center registers 115° to 120°F [45° to 49°C], 3 to 4 minutes longer.

5 Using a wide spatula, transfer the fillets to warmed dinner plates. Remove the herbs from the salmon and arrange two lemon slices on each plate. Serve immediately.

SALMON
GRILLED ON A BED OF HERBS

Serves 4

Here, the salmon cooks up sweet and smoky due to the aromatic herbs. This technique also takes the fear out of grilling fish, because the herbs keep the salmon from sticking to the grill grate. I make this in the summertime, when my thyme and rosemary plants have grown big and bushy with plenty of sprigs to spare. The salmon is terrific served with a mixed grill of zucchini and other summer squashes drizzled with pesto. Or, I make a grain or pasta salad chock-full of diced bell peppers, green or red onions, cherry tomatoes, and zucchini and toss it with an herby citrus dressing.

SALMON
WRAPPED IN CEDAR-WOOD SHEETS

Serves 4

Cedar sheets, rather than whole planks, are great for grilling individual portions of fish, especially fish like salmon and halibut that tend to stick to the grill grate. The technique is easy for a weeknight meal and is an eye-catching presentation for entertaining. Cedar sheets are pliable, smooth, and paper-thin. They come in large squares, just the right size to enclose a single serving. The sheets must be soaked in water to make them pliable enough to roll and tie for grilling. The soaking also minimizes charring of the wood. You can secure the cedar packages in a few different ways. If I have long green onion tops or leek greens on hand, I tie them like string around the rolled sheet. I have also used silicone rubber bands, which I buy at cookware stores. Or, I use kitchen twine that I soak in water along with the cedar sheets. Look for cedar grilling sheets at kitchenware stores, at hardware stores selling grills and grill accessories, or online.

4 center-cut salmon fillets, about 6 oz [170 g] each, skin and pin bones removed

Fine sea salt

Freshly ground black pepper

3 Tbsp extra-virgin olive oil

1 Tbsp fresh lemon juice, plus 1 lemon, cut into 8 paper-thin slices

1 Tbsp finely minced fresh oregano

1 tsp minced garlic

Pinch of cayenne pepper

Long green tops from 4 green onions

You will also need

4 large cedar grilling sheets, each about 8 in [20 cm] square

1 Remove the salmon from the refrigerator 30 minutes before grilling to bring it to room temperature. Pat dry with paper towels.

2 Submerge the cedar grilling sheets in a pan of warm water until pliable, 15 to 20 minutes.

3 Meanwhile, prepare a medium fire in a charcoal grill or preheat a gas grill to medium.

4 Season the salmon fillets on all sides with salt and black pepper. In a small bowl, combine the olive oil, lemon juice, oregano, garlic, and cayenne and mix well. Rub the oil mixture all over the salmon fillets. Arrange two lemon slices, overlapping them slightly, on the flesh side of each fillet.

5 Place the soaked cedar sheets on a work surface. Place a salmon fillet, skinned-side down, in the center of each sheet, parallel to the grain of the wood. Cut eight long strips from the tops of the green onions to use as ties. Working with one cedar sheet at a time, bring up the sides to encase the piece of salmon, forming a tube and overlapping the edges if possible. Wrap a long strip of green onion around the tube about one-third of the way down from the top edge and carefully tie it to secure the tube. Wrap another strip of green onion about one-third of the way up from the bottom edge and tie it. Repeat to secure the other packets.

Continued

6   When ready to grill, generously oil the grill grate. Use tongs to arrange the cedar packets, seam-side up, directly over the fire and cover the grill. Grill until the packets begin to smoke and crackle, about 4 minutes. Turn the packets over, re-cover the grill, and "toast" the second side until the salmon is almost opaque throughout but still very moist, or an instant-read thermometer inserted into the center registers 115° to 120°F [45° to 49°C], 3 to 4 minutes longer.

7   Using tongs, transfer each salmon packet to a warmed dinner plate. Cut the green onions with a knife and use tongs to open the packets and unroll the wood sheets, leaving the salmon inside for an attractive presentation. Serve immediately.

BANANA LEAF–WRAPPED GRILLED **SALMON** WITH LEMONGRASS

Serves 4

In many Asian and Latin American cuisines, banana leaves are used to wrap foods for steaming and grilling. It's an artful and natural way to enclose foods, protecting them from direct heat and sealing in moisture. In addition, the leaves impart a subtle grassy flavor. Be sure to wipe off the whitish coating on the leaves thoroughly before using them for wrapping. Refreeze the extra banana leaves in the package; they're handy to have on hand for grilling other fish that tend to stick to the grill grate, such as halibut and cod. If you have access to fresh fig leaves, they will work equally well for wrapping the fish. The directions for this recipe are long, but I wanted to give detailed instructions on how to wrap the fish to ensure success.

4 center-cut salmon fillets, about 6 oz [170 g] each, skin and pin bones removed

1 lemongrass stalk

2 green onions, white part coarsely chopped and green tops thinly sliced crosswise

2 large garlic cloves, smashed with the side of a chef's knife

1 Tbsp finely chopped fresh cilantro stems, plus 8 sprigs for garnish

1 Tbsp peeled and finely grated fresh ginger

1 Thai bird chile, stemmed and halved lengthwise

1 Tbsp fresh lime juice, plus 4 lime wedges

2 tsp sugar

2 tsp fine sea salt

½ tsp freshly ground black pepper

You will also need

9 pieces frozen banana leaf, 6 by 10 in [15 by 25 cm] each, thawed (see Cook's Note)

1 Remove the salmon from the refrigerator 30 minutes before grilling to bring it to room temperature. Pat dry with paper towels.

2 Trim off the root end from the lemongrass stalk, then cut off and discard the tough green tops. You should have a bulb about 4 in [10 cm] long. Peel away the tough outer leaves, cut the bulb crosswise into ½-in [12-mm] pieces, and then smash the pieces with the side of a chef's knife. Drop the pieces into a food processor. Add the white part of the green onions along with the garlic, cilantro stems, ginger, chile, lime juice, sugar, salt, and pepper and pulse until finely minced, stopping to scrape down the sides of the work bowl once or twice.

3 Place the salmon fillets, skinned-side down, on a work surface. Using a sharp knife, lightly score the top side of each fillet, cutting no more than ⅛ in [3 mm] deep and making diagonal cuts about 1 in [2.5 cm] apart. Place the fillets, scored-side up, in a single layer in a glass or ceramic baking dish. Using a rubber spatula, coat the scored side of each fillet with the lemongrass mixture, dividing it equally. (The cuts will allow the mixture to penetrate the fish.) Cover and refrigerate for 1 hour.

4 Prepare a medium-hot fire in a charcoal grill or preheat a gas grill to medium-high.

5 While the grill is heating, wipe each banana-leaf piece clean with a damp paper towel, removing all of the whitish dusty coating. Using two leaf pieces, arrange one piece horizontally and the other one vertically, in the shape of a cross. Place a fillet, marinated-side up, in the center, where the pieces cross.

Working carefully (the leaves tear easily), bring the top of the vertical piece over to cover the fish, tucking it under the bottom of the fillet. Bring the bottom piece up and fold it over the top. Hold it in place with one hand, if needed, while you bring the left side of the horizontal leaf up and over the fillet, tucking it underneath. Repeat on the right side to enclose the fish in a rectangular parcel. It is fine—desirable, actually—to have the fish enclosed in several layers, which help seal in the juices. Set the packet aside while you wrap the remaining fish fillets the same way.

6 Cut the extra banana leaf into eight long, ribbonlike strips. Use these strips as ties, tying each parcel securely in two places, as if securing a gift.

7 When ready to grill, first create a cool zone by banking the coals to one side of the charcoal grill or by turning off one of the burners of the gas grill. Oil the grill grate. Place the banana-leaf parcels directly over the fire and cover the grill. Grill on one side for 5 minutes. Using a wide spatula, carefully turn the parcels over and re-cover the grill. Cook on the second side for 2 minutes. Move the parcels to the cool side of the grate and continue to cook until an instant-read thermometer inserted through the wrapper into the center of a fillet registers about 120°F [49°C], about 2 minutes longer.

8 Transfer the parcels to a large baking sheet. The outer leaf on each parcel will be brittle, charred, and cracked; carefully remove and discard it. Using a spatula, transfer each parcel to a warmed dinner plate. Open the leaves to reveal the fish and then artfully tuck the edges of the leaves underneath the fish. Garnish each serving with a couple of cilantro sprigs and place a lime wedge next to each fillet. Serve immediately.

COOK'S NOTE

Banana leaves are available in the frozen-foods section of many Asian and Latin American markets. I have occasionally seen them fresh in the produce aisle. The leaves are usually imported from Thailand or the Philippines and come in 16-oz [454-g] packages. Partially thaw the package (this takes only a few minutes) and remove as much as you need for the recipe. Reseal the package, pressing out all the air, and freeze the remainder for later use. They will keep for several months.

ASIAN **SALMON** BURGERS WITH GREEN ONION–SOY MAYONNAISE

Serves 4

Here is a healthful alternative to traditional beef burgers. Packed with ginger, garlic, green onions, and cilantro, these salmon burgers are light, juicy, and look gorgeous on a toasted bun smeared with the green onion–soy mayonnaise. The recipe calls for grilling the burgers, but on a rainy or cold day, they can be panfried with a little oil, browning up beautifully. However, when the salmon burgers are grilled, they have an added smoky flavor and great-looking grill marks. In the summer, make these for a backyard barbecue. The recipe can be easily doubled or tripled for a crowd, and all the prep can be done ahead. The salmon mixture can also be turned into cocktail food by rolling small-meatball-size nuggets and serving the flavored mayonnaise as a dipping sauce.

GREEN ONION–SOY MAYONNAISE

½ cup [120 ml] mayonnaise

1 green onion, including green tops, quartered lengthwise and thinly sliced crosswise

2 tsp soy sauce

1 tsp fresh lemon juice

One 1½-lb [680-g] salmon fillet, skin and pin bones removed, cut into 1-in [2.5-cm] pieces

2 Tbsp chopped fresh cilantro

1 Tbsp peeled and minced fresh ginger

1 Tbsp minced garlic

2 green onions, including 2 in [5 cm] of green tops, halved lengthwise and thinly sliced crosswise

2 Tbsp soy sauce

1½ Tbsp fresh lemon juice

1 tsp fine sea salt

½ cup [50 g] cracker meal

2 large eggs, lightly beaten

2 Tbsp grapeseed or other neutral oil

4 sesame hamburger buns, split

4 lettuce leaves

1 **TO MAKE THE MAYONNAISE:** In a small bowl, combine the mayonnaise, green onion, soy sauce, and lemon juice and mix well. Cover and refrigerate for up to 3 days.

2 Put the salmon in a food processor and pulse until coarsely ground, stopping and scraping down the sides of the work bowl once or twice. (Watch carefully, as it's easy to go from chopped salmon to a mashed paste in seconds.) Transfer the salmon to a medium bowl. Add the cilantro, ginger, garlic, green onions, soy sauce, lemon juice, and salt. Using a rubber spatula, mix until well blended. Stir in the cracker meal and then add the eggs, mixing well.

3 Divide the salmon mixture into four equal portions. Shape each portion into a patty 1 in [2.5 cm] thick and place the patties on a plate. Cover and refrigerate for at least 20 minutes before grilling. (The patties can be prepared up to 8 hours ahead and refrigerated in a covered container.)

4 Meanwhile, prepare a medium-hot fire in a charcoal grill or preheat a gas grill to medium-high.

5 When ready to grill, generously oil the grill grate. Brush the patties on both sides with the grapeseed oil. Place the patties directly over the fire and sear on one side, 3 to 4 minutes. Turn and sear on the second side until almost cooked through, 3 to 4 minutes longer. Place the buns, cut-side down, on the grill to toast during the last minute of grilling.

6 Serve the salmon burgers on the toasted buns with the lettuce and flavored mayonnaise.

GRILLED **SALMON** TACOS WITH CHIPOTLE SAUCE

Serves 6

This is a variation of a recipe that appeared in my first salmon cookbook. I heard from many readers that the grilled salmon tacos were one of their family's favorite recipes. That's not surprising, of course, because if your children love tacos and are happy to eat salmon, this recipe is certain to be a winner. For this book, I decided to update the recipe with a different spice rub. I call this my go-to spice rub because it is equally delicious rubbed on salmon, shrimp, pork, chicken, lamb, beef, buffalo, and even tofu. I always double the rub recipe and keep it in an airtight jar on my pantry shelf, ready for quick-fix weeknight meals like this one.

CHIPOTLE SAUCE

1 cup [240 ml] mayonnaise

3 Tbsp buttermilk or sour cream

2 canned chipotle chiles in adobo sauce, minced

2 Tbsp minced fresh cilantro

¼ tsp fine sea salt

Twelve 6- to 8-in [15- to 20-cm] corn tortillas

One 1½-lb [680-g] salmon fillet, skin on and scaled, pin bones removed

2 Tbsp extra-virgin olive oil

3 Tbsp Diane's Go-To Spice Rub (recipe follows)

½ small head cabbage or iceberg or romaine lettuce, cored and finely shredded

3 green onions, including green tops, quartered lengthwise and cut crosswise into 1-in [2.5-cm] lengths

3 Tbsp fresh lime juice

2 ripe tomatoes, halved crosswise, cored, seeded, and finely chopped

1 **TO MAKE THE CHIPOTLE SAUCE:** In a small bowl, combine the mayonnaise, buttermilk, chipotle chiles, cilantro, and salt and mix well. Cover and refrigerate until ready to use, or for up to 3 days.

2 Position a rack in the center of the oven and preheat the oven to 250°F [120°C]. Prepare a medium fire in a charcoal grill or preheat a gas grill to medium.

3 Place the tortillas in a covered heatproof container or sealed aluminum foil packet. Warm the tortillas in the oven for 15 minutes before serving.

4 Arrange the salmon, skin-side up, on a rimmed baking sheet. Generously oil the skin side of the fillet with 1 Tbsp of the olive oil. Turn the fillet over and oil the flesh side with the remaining 1 Tbsp olive oil. Rub the spice rub into the flesh.

5 When ready to grill, generously oil the grill grate. Place the salmon, skin-side up, directly over the fire. Cover the grill and cook the salmon until beautiful grill marks are etched across the underside of the fillet, about 3 minutes. Turn the fillet skin-side down and re-cover the grill. Cook until the salmon is almost opaque throughout but still very moist, or an instant-read thermometer inserted into the center registers 115° to 120°F [45° to 49°C], 3 to 4 minutes longer. Using a wide spatula, transfer the fillet to a cutting board and let cool slightly.

6 In a medium serving bowl, toss together the cabbage, green onions, and lime juice. Place the tomatoes in a small serving bowl. Slice the salmon crosswise (against the grain) into 12 equal strips. Lift the salmon off its skin and arrange the strips on a warmed serving plate. Transfer the warm tortillas to a separate warmed serving plate.

7 Invite each diner to assemble his or her own tacos. Spread a generous spoonful of the sauce down the middle of a tortilla, arrange a strip of salmon on top, spoon a small mound of the cabbage mixture atop the salmon, and garnish with some tomatoes.

DIANE'S GO-TO SPICE RUB

Makes about 1¼ cups [185 g]

¼ cup [55 g] fine sea salt

¼ cup [50 g] firmly packed dark brown sugar

3 Tbsp ground cumin

2 Tbsp freshly ground black pepper

2 Tbsp sweet paprika

2 Tbsp dried thyme, crushed

2 Tbsp chili powder

1 Tbsp ground coriander

2 tsp ground cinnamon

In a small bowl, combine the salt, brown sugar, cumin, pepper, paprika, thyme, chili powder, coriander, and cinnamon and mix well. Transfer to a jar with a tight-fitting lid and store away from heat and light for up to 6 months.

SALMON
SKEWERS WITH AVOCADO-EDAMAME-WASABI MASH

Serves 4

These colorful salmon skewers, which include squares of red bell pepper and lengths of green onion, take on an Asian fusion profile with bright hits of garlic, ginger, and cilantro. Instead of serving the salmon on a bed of rice—which would also be very good—I've created a chunky, bold-flavored avocado mash as the accompaniment. Lime juice and wasabi spike the creaminess of the avocado, and edamame and chives add flavor and texture. It's a vibrant combination paired with cold beer or a crisp white wine for summer entertaining.

MARINADE

½ cup [120 ml] extra-virgin olive oil

2 Tbsp Asian sesame oil

¼ cup [7 g] minced fresh cilantro

2 large garlic cloves, minced

1 Tbsp peeled and minced fresh ginger

1 tsp fine sea salt

One 1¾-lb [800-g] center-cut salmon fillet, skin and pin bones removed, cut into 1¼-in [3-cm] cubes

AVOCADO-EDAMAME-WASABI MASH

1 cup [150 g] frozen shelled edamame

2 tsp fine sea salt

2 large, ripe Hass avocados, halved, pitted, peeled, and diced

2 Tbsp fresh lime juice

1½ Tbsp wasabi paste

1½ Tbsp finely snipped fresh chives

2 large red bell peppers, seeded, deribbed, and cut into 1-in [2.5-cm] squares (about 32 pieces)

4 green onions, including green tops, cut into 1-in [2.5-cm] lengths (about 32 pieces)

Extra-virgin olive oil for brushing

1 lime, cut into wedges

You will also need

Eight 10-in [25-cm] bamboo skewers

1 **TO MAKE THE MARINADE:** In a medium bowl, combine the olive oil, sesame oil, cilantro, garlic, ginger, and salt and mix well.

2 Add the salmon cubes to the marinade and toss gently to coat on all sides. Cover and set aside at room temperature for up to 45 minutes. (The salmon can be covered and refrigerated for up to 2 hours. Remove from the refrigerator 30 minutes before grilling.)

3 Submerge the bamboo skewers in water for at least 30 minutes, then drain.

4 **WHILE THE SALMON IS MARINATING, MAKE THE MASH:** Fill a small saucepan two-thirds full of water and bring to a boil over high heat. Add the edamame and ½ tsp of the salt and boil for 3 minutes. Drain in a colander and rinse under cold running water. Drain again and blot with paper towels to remove excess moisture.

5 In a medium bowl, using a fork, mash half of the avocado with the lime juice, wasabi paste, and remaining 1½ tsp salt. Fold in the remaining avocado, the edamame, and chives. Taste and adjust the seasoning. Press a sheet of plastic wrap directly onto the surface of the mash, forcing out any air pockets. Set aside until ready to serve.

6 Prepare a medium-hot fire in a charcoal grill or preheat a gas grill to medium-high.

7 Thread a cube of salmon onto a skewer. Follow the salmon with a piece of bell pepper and then a piece of green onion. Repeat the lineup three more times, then load the remaining skewers the same way. Arrange the skewers on a rimmed baking sheet and brush them with olive oil.

8 When ready to grill, generously oil the grill grate. Place the skewers directly over the fire and cover the grill. Cook the skewers on the first side until the salmon begins to color with grill marks, about 4 minutes. Turn the skewers and re-cover the grill. Cook until the salmon is almost opaque throughout but still very moist, about 4 minutes longer.

9 Divide the avocado mash evenly among four warmed dinner plates, mounding it in the center of each plate. Top each mound with two skewers and serve immediately. Pass the lime wedges at the table.

CHAPTER 7:
SECOND HELPINGS

Some folks groan at the sight of leftovers. Not me! Leftovers make me happy. They become building blocks for a creative endeavor in the kitchen. And I consider leftover salmon in my refrigerator a treasure.

At the tail end of writing this cookbook, I remember two weeks in particular when my husband was out of town and I was home alone. A daylong marathon of recipe testing yielded many tasty results and also many leftovers. Here was my chance to work on creative leftover recipes. I regard every meal of the day as a welcome opportunity to eat salmon, and this chapter reflects that way of thinking.

For a weekend breakfast or brunch, I heartily recommend Salmon Hash with Yukon Gold Potatoes and Herbs (page 128) served piping hot directly from the frying pan. Or, make it an eggs-focused brunch with my fishy play on eggs Benedict. Poached Eggs and Smoked Salmon on Tapenade Mayonnaise–Smeared Bread (page 131) skips the traditional ham in favor of salmon and replaces the English muffins with toasted artisanal bread spread with a tapenade-flavored mayonnaise. And the runny egg yolk, rather than hollandaise, becomes the sauce.

Any day I open a lunch box or picnic basket containing Salmon Bánh Mi (page 137) or Salmon Salad Rolls (page 134) is a bonus day for me. Each gives leftover salmon an Asian twist, one in the form of an inspired Vietnamese-style sandwich and the other in a particularly light version of rice paper–wrapped spring rolls. Both are easy to put together.

Four recipes in this chapter make weeknight dinners a breeze. I am especially fond of main-course salads in the summer, and here leftover salmon is transformed into a Salmon Caesar Salad (page 133) in less than a half hour. In August, when corn is fresh at the farmers' market, I make Chunky Salmon, Corn, and Potato Chowder (page 141) that nour-ishes and satisfies as a main course, even on a warm evening. Accenting a rice or pasta dish with salmon and bright citrus flavors is something my family craves. Two favorites are included here: Salmon Risotto with a Cilantro and Orange Gremolata (page 140) and Farfalle Pasta with Salmon, Lemon, and Greens (page 138).

SALMON
HASH WITH YUKON GOLD POTATOES AND HERBS

Serves 4 to 6

Make this hash for a weekend brunch or an easy weeknight supper. For supper, I like to serve it with a tossed green salad or a steamed vegetable and crusty bread. You wouldn't get an argument from me if you decided to replace the butter in the recipe with bacon fat! Or, you could cook half a dozen slices of bacon in the frying pan first, cook the potatoes in the rendered fat, and then chop the bacon and add it to the pot just before serving. For a more protein-packed bowl, top each serving with a poached egg. To kick up the heat, toss in some chopped jalapeño chile with the celery.

4 Tbsp [55 g] unsalted butter

2 lb [910 g] red-skinned, Yukon gold, or Yellow Finn potatoes, peeled and cut into ½-in [12-mm] dice

1 large yellow onion, cut into ½-in [12-mm] dice

2 stalks celery, halved lengthwise, then cut crosswise into slices ½ in [12 mm] thick

1 Tbsp chopped fresh dill

2 tsp minced fresh thyme

1 tsp fine sea salt

½ tsp freshly ground black pepper

3 cups [430 g] coarsely flaked cooked salmon

½ cup [15 g] chopped fresh flat-leaf parsley

Hot-pepper sauce for serving

1 In a 12-in [30.5-cm] frying pan, preferably cast iron, melt the butter over medium heat and swirl to coat the bottom of the pan. Add the potatoes and onion and sauté just until coated with the butter, about 1 minute. Cover and cook to steam the potatoes until they are almost fork-tender, about 7 minutes. Add the celery, stir briefly, and then re-cover and cook for 3 minutes longer. Uncover the pan, increase the heat to medium-high, and add the dill, thyme, salt, and pepper. Cook, stirring frequently, until the potatoes are lightly browned, 15 to 20 minutes.

2 Add the salmon and parsley and cook just until the salmon is heated through. Using a heat-resistant rubber spatula, stir the mixture gently, being careful not to break up the salmon pieces. Taste and adjust the seasoning. Serve immediately, passing the hot-pepper sauce at the table.

POACHED EGGS AND SMOKED SALMON ON TAPENADE MAYONNAISE— SMEARED BREAD

Serves 4

Although many folks want a weekend breakfast or brunch to be on the sweet side, with pancakes or waffles, I typically head in a savory direction. I love the combination of an earthy, rich tapenade mayonnaise smeared on a slice of grilled olive bread, topped with some smoked salmon and a perfectly poached egg. When you cut into the egg, the runny yolk soaks into the crusty bread. Each bite is a savory delight, especially with the addition of smoked salmon. No rich hollandaise sauce is needed here; the runny yolk is the perfect sauce.

TAPENADE MAYONNAISE

6 Tbsp [90 ml] mayonnaise

1½ Tbsp minced fresh flat-leaf parsley

1 Tbsp black olive tapenade

Freshly ground black pepper

8 slices black- or green-olive ciabatta, each ¾ in [2 cm] thick

Extra-virgin olive oil for brushing

16 thin slices smoked salmon (lox) or hot-smoked salmon (see page 62)

8 large eggs

1 tsp distilled white vinegar or fresh lemon juice

1 tsp fine sea salt

1½ Tbsp minced fresh flat-leaf parsley

Freshly ground black pepper

1 **TO MAKE THE MAYONNAISE:** In a small bowl, combine the mayonnaise, parsley, tapenade, and a few grinds of pepper and mix well. Set aside.

2 Heat an indoor grill or a stove-top grill pan or ridged griddle until hot. Brush both sides of each bread slice with a little olive oil. Grill the bread on both sides until nice grill marks appear. Set aside.

3 Pour water to a depth of about 2 in [5 cm] into a large, straight-sided sauté pan and bring to a boil over high heat. While the water is heating, spread each slice of grilled bread on one side with some of the prepared mayonnaise, then lay two salmon slices on top of each bread slice. Divide the bread evenly among warmed plates. Set aside.

4 Crack each egg into a separate small bowl. (I use little ramekins or Pyrex cups.) Line a large, flat plate with a double thickness of paper towel. When the water is boiling, add the vinegar and salt. Adjust the heat so the water is at a simmer, not a rolling boil. Carefully slip the eggs, one at a time, into the water. After 2 or 3 minutes, use a slotted spoon to lift an egg to see if the white has completely set. If it has, one at a time, remove the eggs with the slotted spoon and set them on the prepared plate. Working quickly, use kitchen shears or a paring knife to trim any ragged edges or "tails" from the whites.

5 Set a poached egg on each slice of prepared bread. Garnish each open-face sandwich with a generous sprinkling of the parsley and a couple of grinds of pepper. Serve immediately.

SMOKED **SALMON** FRITTATA WITH GOAT CHEESE AND GREENS

Serves 6 to 8

Learn to make a frittata and you'll have in your repertoire a recipe for many occasions: a brunch for family or friends, a simple supper, or even a picnic main course. You don't need to master a fancy folding technique, such as you do for an omelet, and the opportunity for improvisation with ingredients is infinite. To the basic combination of onions, potatoes, and eggs thinned with a little milk, I have added salmon, spinach, goat cheese, and herbs. Swap out and use other herbs or greens, if desired. And to serve a smaller number, cut the recipe in half and use an 8-in [20-cm] frying pan.

3 Tbsp extra-virgin olive oil	¼ cup [7 g] chopped fresh dill
1 small yellow onion, cut into ½-in [12-mm] dice	1½ tsp fine sea salt
	Freshly ground black pepper
12 oz [340 g] red-skinned potatoes, peeled and cut into ½-in [12-mm] dice	3 oz [85 g] baby spinach
	8 oz [230 g] alder-smoked salmon (see page 62) or other hot-smoked salmon, skin removed and flaked into bite-size pieces
12 large eggs	
½ cup [120 ml] milk	
¼ cup [7 g] chopped fresh flat-leaf parsley	3 oz [85 g] fresh goat cheese

1 In a 12-in [30.5-cm] ovenproof frying pan, preferably nonstick, heat the olive oil over medium heat and swirl to coat the bottom of the pan. Add the onion and potatoes and sauté, stirring occasionally, until the onion softens, about 4 minutes. Turn the heat to medium-low, cover the pan, and cook the onion mixture, stirring occasionally, until the onion and potatoes are tender and beginning to brown, about 10 minutes longer. Turn the heat to low if the onions are browning too quickly.

2 Meanwhile, position an oven rack about 3 in [7.5 cm] from the heat source and preheat the broiler.

3 In a large bowl, whisk together the eggs and milk until thoroughly combined. Whisk in the parsley, dill, and salt and season with pepper. Set aside.

4 As soon as the potatoes are tender, add the spinach and stir until it wilts. Pour in the egg mixture and stir in the salmon. Cook over medium-low heat until the frittata is set on the bottom and around the edges, about 4 minutes. As the frittata is cooking, using a spatula, lift one edge of the frittata and tilt the pan a little so the uncooked eggs flow under the set edge. Repeat this at different places around the edge of the frittata.

5 When the eggs are two-thirds cooked—set around the edges but still runny toward the center—pinch off little globs of goat cheese and scatter them evenly over the top of the frittata, poking them lightly into the eggs but keeping them visible. Place the frittata under the broiler. Broil until the top is golden brown and the eggs are set but still moist, about 3 minutes.

6 Allow the frittata to rest for 5 to 10 minutes, then slice into six to eight wedges. Serve immediately.

SALMON CAESAR SALAD

Serves 4

I try to think strategically about my family's weeknight meals, and this recipe is a good example of my planning methods. Most summer weekends, we fire up the grill and cook dinner. While the grill is hot, I like to cook extra salmon for a future meal, and for this recipe that means four grilled salmon fillets as leftovers. That makes this main-course Caesar salad an ideal weeknight meal. With cooked salmon in the refrigerator, it's easy to whisk together a garlic-fueled creamy Caesar dressing, cube a leftover baguette for making croutons, and tear up some romaine hearts. I prefer to use hearts of romaine because the inner leaves are so much crunchier than the outer leaves of a big head. If the hearts are small, you will need three or four hearts total. I like big Caesar salads, so I am always generous with the amount of greens.

DRESSING

1 Tbsp minced garlic

2 oil-packed anchovy fillets, patted dry and minced

¾ tsp fine sea salt

2 Tbsp fresh lemon juice

1 large pasteurized egg (see Cook's Note)

½ cup [120 ml] extra-virgin olive oil

⅓ cup [30 g] freshly grated Parmesan cheese, preferably Parmigiano-Reggiano

2 cups [220 g] croutons

2 to 3 large hearts of romaine lettuce, torn into bite-size pieces

4 grilled salmon fillets, about 5 oz [140 g] each, skin removed

Freshly grated Parmesan cheese, preferably Parmigiano-Reggiano, for garnish

Freshly ground black pepper

1 **TO MAKE THE DRESSING:** In a small bowl, whisk together the garlic, anchovies, salt, and lemon juice. Add the egg and whisk the dressing until thick, about 1 minute. Slowly drizzle in the olive oil, whisking vigorously to emulsify. Whisk in the cheese. Taste and adjust the seasoning. (The dressing can also be made in a blender or food processor.)

2 Pour half of the dressing into the bottom of an oversize bowl. Add the croutons and toss them in the dressing until thoroughly coated. Add the lettuce and the remaining dressing and toss just until coated.

3 Divide the salad evenly among dinner-size plates. Place a salmon fillet in the center, on top of the salad, and garnish with a dusting of cheese and a grind or two of pepper. Serve immediately.

COOK'S NOTE

To be on the safe side, when using raw eggs in a recipe, use either very fresh, store-bought eggs with clean intact shells and a "pasteurized" label on the carton, or buy your eggs directly from a farmer whose eggs come from pastured poultry (hens who are allowed to roam in pasture as nature intended). If you prefer not to use a raw egg in the dressing, add an additional 1 Tbsp olive oil in place of the egg.

SALMON
SALAD ROLLS

*Makes 8 salad rolls;
serves 8 as an appetizer
or first course*

Flavorful, healthful, and beautiful
to look at, these salad rolls make
perfect appetizers, an unusual first
course to kick off an Asian meal, a
great lunch-box addition, or easy
picnic fare for a summer outing. And
with leftover salmon on hand, they
are quick to put together. What goes
into the salad roll depends on what
you like and what you have on hand.
Sometimes I use watercress instead
of pea shoots, add shredded carrots,
and use mint instead of cilantro. The
dipping sauce is terrific, but if you
are short on time, bottled peanut
sauce will work, too.

HOISIN-PEANUT DIPPING SAUCE

2 Tbsp chunky natural
peanut butter, warmed
slightly to soften

¼ cup [60 ml] hoisin sauce

¼ cup [60 ml] water

1 Tbsp Asian fish sauce, preferably Vietnamese nuoc mam

1 tsp peeled and minced
fresh ginger

¼ tsp red pepper flakes

2 oz [55 g] dried rice vermicelli
(see Cook's Note)

8 round rice paper wrappers,
about 9 in [23 cm] in diameter
(see Cook's Note)

2 oz [55 g] pea shoots
(see Cook's Note)

One 12-oz [340-g] piece grilled
or broiled salmon fillet, skin
removed, cut into 8 long strips

4 green onions, including
green tops, halved lengthwise,
then cut crosswise into
4-in [10-cm] lengths

24 sprigs fresh cilantro

1 TO MAKE THE DIPPING SAUCE: In a small bowl, combine the
peanut butter, hoisin, water, fish sauce, ginger, and red pepper
flakes and mix well. Cover and set aside until ready to serve.
(The sauce will keep in the refrigerator for up to 3 days.)

2 Bring a small saucepan filled with water to a boil over high
heat. Remove from the heat, add the rice vermicelli, and let
soak until tender, 5 to 10 minutes. Drain in a colander, rinse
under cold running water, drain again, and pat dry.

3 Have ready a large bowl of warm water, a clean dry linen
towel, a platter, and the rice paper wrappers. Dip a wrapper
into the water for about 5 seconds, turning to dampen both
sides, and then transfer to the towel. You will use one-eighth
of each ingredient for each roll. To assemble the first roll, lay
a small portion of pea shoots horizontally on the bottom third
of the dampened wrapper. Top with a small mound of noodles,
spreading them horizontally. Place a salmon strip, two pieces
of green onion, and three cilantro sprigs horizontally on top.
Roll the edge of the wrapper nearest you over the filling, creat-
ing a tight cylinder. Roll it halfway over again and then fold
in the sides of the cylinder, envelope style. Continue rolling
the wrapper, always keeping the filling tightly packed, into a
finished cylinder. Place the roll, seam-side down, on the platter.

Continued

4 Repeat with the remaining rice paper wrappers and filling ingredients. (It is important to roll the ingredients into a snug cylinder. If it is not snug, the filling will fall apart when you cut or bite into the roll.) Cover the rolls with a damp paper towel and then with plastic wrap and set aside at room temperature for up to 2 hours.

5 Cut each salad roll in half on the diagonal. Arrange on a platter or on individual small plates. Serve with little bowls of the dipping sauce.

COOK'S NOTES

Rice vermicelli are thin, round rice-flour noodles that commonly appear in the cuisines of Southeast Asia and southern China. They are often used in soups, salads, spring rolls, and stir-fries. You need only soak them in freshly boiled water for about 5 minutes before use. Look for them in well-stocked supermarkets or in Asian grocery stores.

Sometimes labeled "spring roll wrappers," rice paper wrappers (bánh tráng) are thin, translucent dried sheets made from ground white rice, water, salt, and usually a little tapioca flour. They come in various sizes and shapes (round, square, or triangular) and are softened in warm water before using. They are typically rolled around fillings and then served fresh or deep-fried. Look for them in well-stocked supermarkets or in Asian grocery stores.

Pea shoots (doumiao) are the delicate, crisp tendrils and small, tender leaves of pea plants, typically snow peas and less commonly English peas. They taste like a cross between peas and spinach, with a hint of spicy watercress. Look for pea shoots in the produce section of natural foods stores or Asian markets, and pinch off and discard any tough tendrils before using. If the pea shoots appear to have many tough tendrils, buy extra to ensure you have enough after trimming.

SALMON
BÁNH MI

Makes 4 sandwiches

Let's talk about all the possible variations for this dynamite sandwich! When I make Asian salmon burgers, I like to make small balls from any leftover salmon mixture and panfry them. I smear the bánh mi rolls with the same green onion–soy mayonnaise I use for the burgers, and then I layer the rolls with the salmon balls, pickled carrots, jalapeños, cucumber, and cilantro. Sometimes, instead of just carrots, I pickle a combination of daikon and carrots. I've used other flavored mayonnaise in the sandwiches, too, such as the chipotle sauce on page 122 and the citrus Sriracha sauce on page 69, both especially good with leftover grilled salmon. Use mint or arugula instead of cilantro, and if you don't want the heat of the jalapeños, use strips of sweet bell pepper in place of the chiles. These sandwiches are great wrapped in parchment or wax paper and taken along on a picnic.

QUICK PICKLED CARROTS

½ cup [120 ml] distilled white vinegar

½ cup [100 g] sugar

½ tsp fine sea salt

1 large carrot, peeled and cut into matchsticks

4 bánh mi or crusty rolls

12 oz [340 g] cooked salmon meatballs (made from the salmon mixture for Asian salmon burgers on page 120) or hot-smoked or grilled salmon, cut into long strips

Mayonnaise for spreading

Fine sea salt

Freshly ground black pepper

1 to 2 large jalapeño chiles, stemmed and thinly sliced, seeds removed if desired

1 English cucumber, trimmed and cut into thin rounds

½ bunch fresh cilantro, large stems removed

1 **TO MAKE THE PICKLED CARROTS:** In a small bowl, combine the vinegar, sugar, and salt and stir until the sugar and salt have dissolved. Add the carrot and press down to submerge in the pickling liquid. Let stand for 20 minutes while you prepare the sandwich filling. (The pickled carrots can be made ahead, covered, and refrigerated for up to 1 month.) Drain the carrots well before using.

2 If needed, recrisp the rolls in a 300°F [150°C] oven for 5 minutes. At the same time, warm the salmon in a covered pan in the oven just to take the chill off, about 10 minutes. Remove the mayonnaise from the refrigerator 15 minutes before using so it isn't refrigerator cold.

3 Using a serrated knife, split a roll lengthwise, cutting almost all the way but not completely through the crust on the backside. Use your fingers to remove some of the crumb from the top cut side of the roll, hollowing out a canoe-shaped cavity the length of the roll. Spread a generous amount of mayonnaise lengthwise down both cut sides. Season the mayonnaise on both sides with a little salt and pepper. Arrange one-fourth of the salmon in a layer along the bottom half of the roll. Add a layer of pickled carrots, followed by some jalapeño and cucumber slices, and then finish with some cilantro. Close the sandwich and cut in half crosswise. Repeat with the remaining rolls and filling ingredients. Serve immediately.

Fine sea salt

1 lb [455 g] farfalle
(bow-tie pasta)

1½ cups [360 ml] heavy
whipping cream

1 garlic clove, lightly smashed

12 oz [340 g] baby spinach,
large stems removed

Grated zest of 1 lemon, plus
¼ cup [60 ml] fresh lemon juice

Freshly ground black pepper

8 oz [230 g] cooked salmon
fillet, skin removed

Freshly grated Parmesan
cheese, preferably Parmigiano-
Reggiano, for serving

FARFALLE PASTA WITH SALMON, LEMON, AND GREENS

Serves 4 to 6

I like to have recipes like this one up my sleeve that I can put together with fresh greens that I purchase and pantry staples that I have on hand, such as dried pasta, garlic, and lemons. Use prewashed baby spinach or buy bushy fresh greens such as kale, chard, or even turnip tops at the farmers' market (or, if you are lucky, pluck them from your garden) and make this dish on a harried weeknight. The sauce comes together in the time it takes to cook the pasta.

1 Fill a large stockpot two-thirds full of water, add 1 Tbsp salt, and bring to a boil over high heat. Add the pasta and stir. Cook the pasta until al dente, 11 to 12 minutes or according to package directions.

2 While the pasta is cooking, pour the cream into a large sauté pan and drop in the garlic. Bring to a boil over medium heat and simmer for 5 minutes. Remove the garlic. Add the spinach, a handful at a time, and stir just until it wilts, about 1 minute. Add the lemon zest, lemon juice, 1 tsp salt, and a few grinds of pepper. Stir to combine and then gently stir in the salmon. Cook just until heated through. Set aside and keep warm.

3 When the pasta is ready, drain it in a colander, reserving ½ cup [120 ml] of the cooking water. Place the pan with the cream mixture over medium heat. Add the pasta to the pan and toss to combine. Add just enough of the reserved pasta water, a little at a time, as needed to moisten. When heated through, remove from the heat.

4 Divide the pasta among warmed shallow pasta bowls and shower with Parmesan cheese. Serve immediately.

SALMON
RISOTTO WITH A CILANTRO AND ORANGE GREMOLATA

Serves 4 as a main course

A divine dinner in just over a half hour! Creamy white risotto dotted with bite-size pieces of salmon is garnished with an herby citrus gremolata. My preference would be to use leftover slow-roasted salmon (see page 96) or poached salmon (see page 63) for this recipe rather than, say, grilled salmon flavored with a robust marinade. The delicate flavor of the salmon will balance nicely with the creaminess of the rice and the brightness of the fresh herbs and orange zest. You don't need to wait for leftover salmon to make this dish for dinner, however. You can start with a raw salmon fillet, cut it into bite-size pieces, and add it at the same time as the cooked salmon is added in the recipe. Simmer it for just a minute longer and it will be cooked through.

CILANTRO AND ORANGE GREMOLATA

⅓ cup [10 g] minced fresh cilantro

2 garlic cloves, minced

Grated zest of 1 orange

5 cups [1.2 L] homemade chicken stock or canned low-sodium chicken broth

3 Tbsp extra-virgin olive oil

⅔ cup [90 g] diced white onion

1½ cups [300 g] Arborio rice

Fine sea salt

½ cup [120 ml] dry white wine

½ cup [120 ml] heavy whipping cream

12 oz [340 g] cooked salmon fillet, skin removed, cut into bite-size pieces

1 cup [160 g] orange or red cherry tomatoes, halved

Freshly ground black pepper

1 **TO MAKE THE GREMOLATA:** In a small bowl, combine the cilantro, garlic, and orange zest and mix well. Set aside.

2 In a 2-qt [2-L] saucepan, bring the chicken stock to a simmer over medium heat. Adjust the heat so the stock barely simmers.

3 In a heavy 4-qt [3.8-L] saucepan, warm the olive oil over medium heat and swirl to coat the bottom of the pan. Add the onion and sauté until translucent but not browned, about 3 minutes. Add the rice and 1 tsp salt and stir until the grains are well coated with the oil, about 1 minute. Add the wine and let it come to a boil. Cook, stirring constantly, until most of the wine is absorbed.

4 Add 2 cups [480 ml] of the stock to the rice and cook, stirring frequently, until the rice has almost completely absorbed the liquid. Adjust the heat so the risotto is kept at a slow simmer. Add the remaining stock, 1 cup [240 ml] at a time, stirring until it is almost fully absorbed before adding more. Reserve ¼ cup [60 ml] of the stock for adding at the end.

5 After about 18 minutes, the rice will be plump, creamy, and cooked through but still slightly chewy. Stir in the cream, and then stir in the salmon, cherry tomatoes, and remaining ¼ cup [60 ml] stock. Stir gently for about 2 minutes, allowing some of the liquid to be absorbed and the salmon and tomatoes to heat through. Season with pepper. Remove the risotto from the heat.

6 Spoon the risotto into warmed shallow pasta bowls and garnish with the gremolata. Serve immediately.